Praise for

ALL ABOUT GLORY

All about Glory is a beautifully and simply
written book, which carries within its
simplicity a vision loaded with the glory
of God. As you read you will find yourself
stopping, underlining and rereading. You will
think. You will ponder. You will wonder. You
will hope. It will gradually dawn on you that
there is far more going on in your life than
you ever dared to dream.

- C Baxter Kruger
Author of *The Shack Revisited*

ALL ABOUT GLORY

WHERE HOPE AND MEANING MEET

DAVID KOWALICK

Godwit
Media

Requests and inquiries concerning reproduction and rights should be addressed to Godwit Media at godwitmin@bigpond.com

Printed in Australia

First Edition: September 2013

Editors: Amanda Hancock, Elise Ruthenbeck, Kristy Schubert
Cover design: Nicole Dunkley
Typesetting: Green Hill Publishing
Publisher: Godwit Media www.godwitmin.com

ISBN 978-0-923392-0-3

In memory of Dan.

Forever young.

FOREWORD

As a child I had to learn the catechism. Here is the first question and answer. "What is man's chief end? Man's chief end is to glorify God and enjoy him forever." Although I quite agree with George MacDonald when he wished that the engineers of the catechism would have "glorified God by going no further," I have to admit that this first question and answer set something of a life-long agenda for me. From the moment that I successfully memorised the question and answer, another emerged: 'How can you *glorify God* and *enjoy* anything?' Looking back over five decades of my life it is clear that this was no mere philosophical question, but one that was a matter of life or death for me. And it was a question that contained myriads of other questions within it, and one that was bound up with enormous, yet subtle assumptions. For me, 'glorifying God' meant obedience to the rule or the law of a distant, yet watching Deity. So I was genuinely mystified. What, pray tell, could glorifying God possibly mean? How could doing 'the God thing' be related to 'joy' of any kind? Seriously?

In *All About Glory*, David Kowalick has done me, and I suspect many others, a great service. He has taken 'glory'

out of the realm of abstractions and external obedience —
where the word 'glory' is largely meaningless and certainly
useless — and placed it within the realm of relationship,
where it becomes profoundly personal, alive and full of
hope. Actually, I should say, he shows us how relationship
has been the true realm of glory and of glorifying all along.
It is a brilliant move, and once seen, it appears clearly and
obviously biblical.

Kowalick defines glory as "the essential nature and reality
of any given thing or person at its fullest and best." To 'glorify'
something then is to reveal its essential character. *Glory* is
the truth of all truths of a person, place, or thing. *Glorifying*
is therefore about this truth being manifested, and thus
known. When John says that Jesus "manifested his glory"
(John 2:11) when he turned the water into wine, he is saying
that the event revealed something essential about the nature
of Jesus himself.

In a few strokes of his pen Kowalick challenges our
assumptions about glory as the honor and honoring of
a distant God to help us see glory as the revelation, the
unveiling, and the manifestation of the character and essential
person. He moves us from a sterile doctors' office where we
are patients, clinically examined and observed and evaluated,
and handed a prescription to obey, into a relationship where
we discover that we are wanted, accepted, even adored, and
thus awakened and inspired to love and live in hope.

Seeing 'glory' as the essence of a person leads Kowalick
into a discussion of the glory of God as the relationship of
knowing, and being known by the Father, Son, and Holy
Spirit. The glory of God is not about legalities and abstract
honor, or about some kind of divine effervescent luminosity.

The glory of God — the essential character and nature of God — is the shockingly beautiful, other-centred, self-giving, serving love of the Father, Son and Holy Spirit. In the words of Malcolm Smith, "God does not love. God *is* love." So thankfully, Kowalick spends a good deal of time helping us behold the glory of the blessed Trinity, helping us see how the Father loves the Son and the Son loves the Father in the freedom of the Holy Spirit.

Such a move alone is worth the time of reading this book, but for Kowalick, seeing the way Jesus and the Holy Spirit and the Father relate, how they love and care and give to one another is only the beginning of the tale to be told. For any talk of the essential character of God carries implications for the whys and wherefores of our existence. The glory of God speaks volumes about *our* glory. And so, this vision of the beautiful relationship of the Father, Son and Spirit — the glory of God — defines the meaning and purpose, and the *glory* of creation and redemption, and indeed it defines *our glory*. We cannot talk about the beauty of the relationship of the Father, Son and Spirit without, at the same time, talking about why God created and redeemed us.

The glory of the Father, Son and Spirit, the shared life of the blessed Trinity, is not the sort of thing that is to be hoarded. This life is to be shared. This is the *why* of creation, and it is *why* Jesus became one of us. As Irenaeus said in the second century of the Church's life, "our Lord Jesus Christ, who did, through his transcendent love, become what we are, that he might bring us to be even what he is himself." The Father's Son became one of us not to parade his glory, but to share it, to give us a place in all that he is, in his essential nature as the Father's beloved Son and the one anointed in the Holy Spirit without measure. The glory of God is the other-centred love, the fellowship, the oneness of the Father, Son and Spirit; and our glory is that we are included. We belong to this life. "Christ in you, the hope of glory" (Col. 1:27).

'Glory,' as it turns out, is not a peripheral topic, but a central one, at the heart of the very being of God, creation, marriage, family, relationships and life. And, as it turns out, the more we follow Kowalick into this vision of God's glory and our glorification in Jesus Christ, the more we find ourselves stunned in awe and wonder and hope along with the early Church.

All about Glory is a beautifully and simply written book, which carries within its simplicity a vision loaded with the glory of God. As you read you will find yourself stopping, underlining and rereading. You will think. You will ponder. You will wonder. You will hope. It will gradually dawn on you that there is far more going on in your life than you ever dared to dream, and as it does you will be glorified, and as you are glorified so will be the Father, Son and Spirit. "When Christ, who is our life, is revealed, then you also will be revealed with Him in glory" (Col. 3:4)

— C. Baxter Kruger, Ph.D., author of *Across All Worlds* and *The Shack Revisited*

CONTENTS

AUTHOR'S PREFACE

Just outside the city where I live there's a walking track up a steep hill. About halfway up, immediately past a particularly steep section of track, somebody has thoughtfully erected a comfortable seat in the shade of a tree. This location offers a brilliant view of the city, framed by the valley and pleasantly offset by the greenery in the foreground. So satisfying is this view that it's very tempting to abandon the ascent right there. It's hard to imagine how it could be much improved on further up the hill. But anyone who has been to the top will tell you it's definitely worth the effort: the view is all the more sublime.

To me, this scenario perfectly captures what we in the Western Church have done with our view of the Gospel. I believe we are stuck halfway up the hill sitting on a comfortable chair called 'The Reformation' which offers a magnificent view of the Gospel framed by 'justification by faith' and pleasantly offset by the grace of God. It's hard to imagine how there could be anything more wonderful than this.

That was pretty much how I felt until I stumbled upon an essay called 'The Weight of Glory' by C.S. Lewis. I already harboured a half-felt suspicion that there was something more to the Gospel than I already recognised, and as I began to soak up the words in that short essay, something like a dam burst inside me. Suddenly the New Testament shone with new light that had me seeing things I'd previously overlooked; the more I looked the more I saw the things I had not seen. It reminded me of the words of the apostle Paul,

> "What no eye has seen, what no ear has heard, and what no human mind has conceived" — the things God has prepared for those that love him — *these are the things God has revealed to us by his Spirit.*
>
> — (1 Corinthians 2: 9-10)

But what exactly is it that 'God has prepared for those that love him,' that the Spirit wants to make known to us? I believe the answer—which this book is mainly about — is *glory*.

Unfortunately, experience has taught me that right about now your interest will be fading with the mention of the word 'glory.' What, after all, does that word even mean? That's the problem with this subject — it can seem so out of reach and unimaginable, and therefore irrelevant. Yet, I would argue, that glory is one of the fundamental cornerstones of the gospel message. It's certainly one of the major sub-texts of the Gospel of John and Paul's epistle to the Romans. But somewhere along the way we seem to have lost sight of this 'view from the top' and have settled for the 'halfway-chair' instead. There's nothing wrong with the view from halfway up, but I urge you: keep going all the way to the top, it's even better than you can imagine!

You may be thinking, "If the subject of glory is so important, then why isn't everyone talking about it? Why isn't it common knowledge?" This was not always the case, for there was a time, in the first centuries of the Church, that the subject of glory was considered essential but somehow we seem to have lost connection with this vital element of the Gospel. Unfortunately, once something is no longer considered essential, it soon becomes poorly understood, unappreciated, and then virtually invisible. But the reverse is just as true — a new found understanding generates interest and appreciation, which in turn makes the invisible visible again.

Have you ever noticed what happens when you buy a new car? All of a sudden you begin to notice the make and model of your new vehicle everywhere. Until then you didn't even know it existed. I believe something like that is true of glory. Once you begin to see its vital significance to the Gospel, and to life, you'll begin to see it everywhere.

The first believers certainly *did* notice glory and back then everyone *was* talking about it. Indeed the New Testament and the writings of the Early Church are full of it! Even in more recent history, there have been some outstanding books and essays put forward by well-known theologians on the subject, including a seven volume work: 'The Glory of the Lord' by Hans Urs von Balthasar, which brilliantly delves into all this and more. This brings me to the reason for writing this book, which is this: to put glory back on the table in a way that can be understood and appreciated.

However, if you are anything like me — which is to say somewhere in the middle bit of the bell-curve of human intelligence — then you might have found the prospect of grappling with academic Christian theology somewhat daunting. I've certainly 'pulled a hammy' in my cerebral cortex plenty of times while attempting to hurdle the obscure terminology of theological books such as these.

The problem with theological books is that they're written by theologians, and the problem with theologians is they're geniuses, and the thing about geniuses is they have no idea what it's like for the rest of us mere mortals. They simply don't know how to communicate with normal people. This book is a hopeful attempt to put in ordinary language some of the amazing things that are otherwise hidden in the impenetrable undergrowth of theological language. I underscore the word *attempt* here because it has been much harder to do than I thought. It turns out that the easier something is to read, the harder it is to write.

This book is a short introduction to the subject of 'glory' — a subject which has gripped my attention for decades. The more I have delved into this subject the more I have come to realize its profound implications for every arena of life. It's in no way a comprehensive or exhaustive look at the subject: it's simply a primer. It's also my intention that some readers will make use of this book as a way of introducing the essentials of Christian faith via the doorway of glory.

After the introductory first chapter, the book is divided into three parts. Part One explores the glory of God, Part Two: glory and humanity, and Part Three: glory in family relationships. I trust you will find it helpful in opening the endless possibilities that this subject leads to, in language that is both meaningful and clear.

In hope and faith,
David Kowalick

1

GLORY

What is Glory?

Sometimes, when you least expect it, and in the most unlikely of places, it happens.

It happened to me one day in the arrivals lounge at Sydney's International Airport.

I was thumbing my way through a dull book while waiting for a friend to arrive. All around the airport were walls of television screens displaying the 1996 Olympic Games to the constant stream of tired travellers. The 1500 metre freestyle swimming final had just begun and one of Australia's favourite sons was taking part.

Kieran Perkins, who'd claimed the gold medal in the previous Olympics, was out to defend his title, but a combination of sickness, injury and a promising crop of younger swimmers all looked set to sideline the former champion. No one expected Kieran to get past the heats. Yet, somehow, he'd scraped into the slow-lane for the final and there he was plunging into the water: all captured on the larger-than-life banks of video vision for all to see.

As Kieran steadily carved his way through the water, I steadily lost interest in my book. Stroke by stroke, second by second, it became increasingly evident that Kieran might just be about to make Olympic history and win the event for an unprecedented second time. A hush fell upon the crowds in the airport as every eye and ear was fixed on the screens and we dared to hope for an impossible victory. Even before the final lap, everybody in the airport was out of their chairs as they urged him on. When, at last, Kieran touched the wall in first place, we all erupted in spontaneous cheering, backslapping, and warm embraces. Tears flowed freely and beaming smiles were evident in every direction — not least of all my own. I'm quite certain that flights were missed that day and others delayed, so mesmerising was the moment of that event.

And there it was — a glimpse of magnificent, unplanned glory.

Over the years I've often reflected on moments like these, and it seems clear to me that 'glimpses of glory' such as these occupy our collective imagination far more than we probably realize. I believe glory is the intangible 'something' we seek in nature, the arts, the sporting arena, worship and close relationships. We can't help but commemorate it, and celebrate it, because ultimately we *need* it. Yet it seems to me we're not entirely certain just what '*it*' really is. We recognise its presence when we encounter it, but where it comes from, or where it's leading to, we hardly know.

Glory is a word I see being used in all kinds of contexts. Unfortunately, we mostly use it in a frivolous way, and I think it might be fair to say we have lost sight of its real meaning.

In the Church, for instance, the word glory is particularly misunderstood and poorly appreciated. It seems most people have only an ethereal notion of glory, thinking of some 'pie in the sky' place that we say people 'passed on to.' Sometimes it's thrown about as an adjective: 'It was a glorious day.' Other times we use it verbally; 'Glory to God for the great things he has done.' Generally, it's used vaguely or flippantly, which is a shame, because 'glory' is a profound word. No definition can really do it justice, but I'll try to put forward a simple biblical idea which might help us rediscover this most important and wonderful truth. Very simply: glory is the essential nature and reality of any given thing or person at its fullest and best.

There are over twenty different words used in the Bible that are translated to 'glory' in the English language. In the Old Testament, the main Hebrew word for glory, *kabod*, means weight or heaviness. The writers were using the word to say something about the substance of a thing. When we feel the weight of something we get an impression of its mass and significance. In the New Testament, the writers mainly used the Greek word *doxa*, which means the apparent worth, 'seeming,' substance, and/or dignity of something.

So, glory can be used to talk about moments when something or somebody is seen as they really are: an unobstructed display of being or reality. When Kieran Perkins won his second gold medal, he was revealed as an extraordinary swimmer and something of the substance of his character was unveiled — that's getting us closer to the way biblical writers used the word. Even the slang phrase 'there he was in all his glory' as a euphemism for nakedness probably uses 'glory' more precisely than the way it's usually used — even in the church. Glory is all about unveiled reality.

Glory is not an achievement or a place we go to. We can grow in appreciation of glory, or we can come to recognise it, but we can't acquire glory. It just is. The fullest and best of each thing doesn't require our observation in order for it to exist. Yet there's another crucial aspect of glory which is often overlooked: the self-revelatory nature of glory. In the Bible, glory is often associated with the idea of radiance or shining splendour, and this certainly captures something of the self-revealing nature of glory. Glory is always showing something to us — it's almost as if it's intentionally pointing us in a certain direction — helping us to 'see.'

Seeing Glory

I'm a birdwatcher, although I hardly blame myself for becoming so. I always imagined birdwatchers to be an eccentric bunch, more than a little detached from reality. The more robust pursuits of fishing and bushwalking had arrested my recreational attention, until my father-in-law, an ardent birdwatcher himself, gave me a pair of binoculars for Christmas one year. I had no idea at the time that this was to be the beginning of a lifelong pursuit of all things bird related.

The binoculars weren't to blame, though. The real protagonist in my unwitting slide into the world of ornithology was a tiny bird known as a Rainbow Bee-eater. I had previously been aware of many of the common and larger birds, but had never really noticed the amazing variety and colour that birds bring to an average suburban garden, let alone the incredible diversity to be encountered in the wild. When my binoculars focussed on that little bird one summer afternoon, everything changed. The vivid hues of electric blue and iridescent orange dazzled me, and the sheer beauty and spritely movements of that otherwise insignificant creature overwhelmed me.

The binoculars gave me new eyes. For the first time, all the nondescript 'little brown birds' which had passed by unnoticed suddenly captivated my attention. The binoculars glorified the birds; they allowed me to see them as they really are. Glory is like that: it's magnificence revealed. So it is with all kinds of glory. The more clearly we 'see' something, the more we appreciate the glory that's there.

We're surrounded by countless kinds of glory if we care to *really* see. There's a whole world of sights, sounds and sensations in every bit of creation. From the rhythm of a river, the feel of sand underfoot, the warmth of the sun, the fragrance of a forest, to the tumult of a storm, the savagery of a lion or the violence of a volcano. Yet all these things — though wonderful — are only the leading edge of glory. There are immeasurable and infinite degrees of glory in all the intangible aspects of creation such as the wonder of friendship, the beauty of music, the mystery of mercy, or the virtue of courage. *Everything* has its own particular degree and kind of glory.

Original glory

All glory originates from God and — in the end — points back to God. God is somehow revealed in the unique glory of every created thing. Ducks, for instance, have 'duck glory.' Duck glory is seen when ducks simply are ducks and do what ducks do. Each species of duck has a distinct contribution to make to our understanding of ducks and every individual adds yet another subtle nuance to overall duck glory. We can understand something of the nature of God in the life of a duck but only to the degree that a duck has the capacity to reveal God as he really is. In this way, creation can be like a pair of binoculars to help us see God behind the glory, but the effect could be magnified even further if we had a telescope.

More Glory

Let's say the more something is like God, the more it can magnify God. Imagine, then, a creature that's actually made in the very image of God, and is able to give us not just binocular vision of God, but telescope vision.

The Bible makes it pretty clear that there's something about human beings that makes them 'telescopically' special. In the Genesis story, we see God review his handiwork at the end of each day of creation with the statement: "It was good." When he created humanity, he called his creation, "very good."(Genesis 1: 31). When humanity was created, creation itself was brought to completion and became fully functional and truly beautiful. Creation with people in it was creation in completion. It was glorious.

Elsewhere, King David is in wonder as he surveys the glories of God's creation and writes,

When I consider your heavens, the work of your fingers,
The moon and the stars, which you have set in place
What is mankind that you are mindful of them,
Human beings that you care for them?

— Psalm 8: 3-4

Most often, when people read this passage, they understand it as David in lament, as if he were saying that humanity is nothing when compared with creation and that he's amazed God would even bother to take thought of humankind — but the exact *opposite* is true! If we read on we discover that God has 'crowned' humanity with 'glory and honor' and has 'made them rulers' over the rest of creation (Psalm 8: 5-9). David is in awe that God has assigned more glory to humanity than to all the stars, mountains, creatures, and everything else in creation.

I'll never forget a particular event at one of my children's school sports days. One of the girls in a running race was severely disabled by spina-bifida and at best she could only hope to shuffle in an ungainly fashion toward the finishing line, so the organisers arranged for her to start in the hundred metre race twenty metres in front of the others. Despite her advantage, the rest of the children soon caught up to her, but instead of dashing past her, they all spontaneously adjusted their speed to keep pace with her to the finish line. Parents and children cheered together as she crossed the finish line beaming a huge smile. I can't find words to fully capture the beauty of that moment. God was in that event. Something profound and wonderful was revealed about God in the actions of human beings that day.

Even More Glory

Have you ever looked at the stars through an astronomer's telescope or gazed at images from the Hubble telescope? It's pretty amazing and we can gain a lot of knowledge about the universe with the aid of these devices. But here's the thing: no matter how much magnification the telescope can muster it doesn't enable us to actually *see* a star. There are stars we *think* we can see that have ceased to exist for thousands of years. What we call stars are actually ancient images of stars and even these images are distorted by cosmic radiation and the dust and pollution of our atmosphere. We would have to actually travel to the star and land on its surface to really *see* the star.

In a similar way we may be able to learn a whole lot about God in the glimpse of a bird's wing, or in human acts of kindness, but even that which is revealed in the better parts of humanity still falls well short of the magnificence we could expect to see in the fully unveiled face of God.

The scriptures tell us that 'No one has ever seen God' (John 1: 18). Although some might argue that Moses, at least, *has* seen God, when he petitioned, "Now show me your glory" (Exodus 33: 18), God said:

> When my glory passes by, I will put you in a cleft in the rock and cover you with my hand until I have passed by. Then I will remove my hand and you will see my back; but my face must not be seen.
>
> — Exodus 33: 22-23

Whichever way you take this story, and its significance, it must be said that Moses did not see the *full* glory of God. He saw *something* of the essential nature of God but did not see the face of God. Moses received the law in his encounter with God and through the law 'the back' of God is revealed. In other words God is glorified by the law, because it reveals his mercy, justice, kindness, integrity and much more besides, but it isn't God in all his fullness.

So where can we see God as he really is?

Glory in Fullness

The apostle Paul in his second letter to the Corinthians gives us a clue when he writes,

> For God, who said, "Let light shine out of darkness," made his light shine in our hearts to give us the light of *the knowledge of God's glory displayed in the face of Christ*.
>
> — 2 Corinthians 4: 6

When we look at the 'face of Jesus Christ,' we're actually looking at the face of God *fully revealed*. Jesus is not just a teacher or prophet — someone with a powerful telescope — he *is* God. Creation can only reflect the glory of God, but Jesus actually *is* God. Jesus Christ is the source of light itself: the pure relationships and perfect love between the Father, Son, and Holy Spirit.

God in Human Flesh

All this would be enough, but there's something more we see when we look at the face of Jesus Christ: we see a *human* face. The God we see in Jesus Christ is so much more than a distant deity in the sky. On the contrary, we discover the God who willingly joins himself to our humanity in his Son, thus making it possible for us to encounter his life and love in a powerfully palpable way.

In Jesus, not only do we see God as he really is, we also get a glimpse of what a truly glorious human being looks like. He gives us a perfect vision of what we *could be*, and this in turn ignites an aching desire in us that we *would be* what we *could be!* As C.S. Lewis explains, this yearning is more than merely wishful thinking:

> Apparently, then, our lifelong nostalgia, our longing to be reunited with something in the universe from which we now feel cut off, to be inside of some door which we have always seen from the outside, is no mere neurotic fancy, but the truest index of our real situation. And to be at last summoned inside would be both glory and honour beyond all our merits and also the healing of that old ache.[i]

This longing for glory is a proper and appropriate desire that perfectly aligns with the designs God has always had for the human race. In becoming human, Jesus has 'summoned us inside' that we might be participants in the glory of God, not just onlookers.

I'm convinced that it was *this* that fuelled the enthusiasm and resolve of the first believers. Take, for instance, these words by the apostle Paul:

> For those God foreknew he also predestined to be conformed to the image of his Son, that he might be the firstborn among

many brothers and sisters. And those he predestined, he also called; those he called, he also justified; those he justified, he also glorified.

— Romans 8: 29

Notice the progression in this passage: it begins with God's premeditated intention from before time, captured in a definitive plan, leading to our personal call, followed up with a transforming restoration, making us fit and ready for the ultimate goal — glorification. As far as Paul is concerned the summit of the hill goes beyond justification to *glorification;* even to the point of being 'conformed to the image of his Son' to such a profound degree that Jesus would be called our 'brother.'

The implications of all this are staggering.

If Jesus is our brother, then that must mean *his Father is our Father,* and knowing God as Father, and relating to him as his child, is what it really means to be glorified because this is the very thing we were originally and purposefully created for. To see God 'as he really is' is to see the Father who not only loves his Son, but also loves *us,* and intentionally comes for us, as a father comes for his children, and the whole creation attests to how beautiful that love is.

Missing the Point

So, if all this is true then why isn't this being proclaimed on every corner, and shouted from the mountain tops? Did we miss a turn somewhere? I think we did.

I want to show you something. It's hidden away in two slightly different translations of Romans 8: 21. In one translation, it says, "…the creation itself also will be delivered from the bondage of corruption into the *glorious liberty* of the children of God."[ii] But another translation has it as, "… the creation itself also will be set free from its slavery to corruption into the *freedom of the glory* of the children of God."[iii] The first translation emphasises the freedom, which is glorious, but the other underscores the glory, which is freeing. Right here we have unearthed what I believe is one of the fundamental 'wrong turns' in Western Christianity. This verse can be legitimately translated either way, so the choice to translate it one way or the other will be largely determined by the partiality of the translator.

As explained in the preface, the church has become so engrossed with the magnificence of justification, and the freedom it brings, that we have overlooked the grand purpose that justification serves — glorification. We are not freed so that we can simply enjoy freedom; rather we are freed so that we can become what we were created to be — children of God!

Mercenary faith

In my family, we have a tradition that whenever I go away, interstate or overseas, I must bring back gifts for my children. The longer I am away and the further I travel, the bigger the gift must be. Consequently, my children are very much in favour of extended trips to far flung locations on the other side of the world.

Some time ago I'd been on one such trip and, upon my return, my wife Catherine told me of the details of a discussion which took place between my children on the way to the airport. My three sons took turns calculating the probable size and value of the gift they would receive.

'I think Daddy will bring a really big present.'

'I think Daddy will bring me a present worth at least twenty dollars.'

And so on.

But my daughter cut right across the basic tenor of this discussion saying, 'I don't care what Daddy brings me. I just want Daddy back.'

I have had the opportunity to observe the church in many countries and denominations and it seems to me we are all rather busy calculating the size and value of the gift that God is giving us — forgiveness of sin, justification, heaven, escape from judgement, and all the other benefits — without seeing what my daughter saw: that the most important thing is not the gifts that come from the relationship, but the person to whom we are relating.

It's a curious thing that in Christian discipleship we are taught, both from the pulpit and by existential suffering, that a man or woman's "life does not consist in an abundance of possessions" (Luke 12: 15), nor of his or her position in life (1 John 2: 16). Suddenly, after a lifetime of gaining this hard won truth, are we then to abandon it in favour of a 'mansion in the sky' and 'streets of gold?' Have you ever assumed that when a beautiful young woman marries an aged but wealthy man, it's only for his money? Sadly, I believe this is exactly the sort of thing many sermons seem to be encouraging. 'Come to Jesus and escape hell' or 'Put your faith in Christ and he will give you peace of mind.' It's as if they're saying, 'Marry Jesus for his money.' This misses everything that's important and true about glory.

The amazing truth is that sharing in the glory of God is the goal of all things: we don't just get to admire the love of God; we get to participate in it! When *this* truth captures our attention, our view of the world dramatically changes. The joy of being fully at one with the Father, and the Son, in fellowship with the Holy Spirit, changes the colour of everything.

As wonderful as all this sounds, believing it is not so easy. The dull grind of our daily existence stunts the reach of our hope, and our sorrow, guilt and shame all conspire to cloud our vision with anger or self-loathing. Sure, these things might be true for those special 'holy' people, but it couldn't possibly have anything to do with ordinary broken people like you and I ... could it?

Yet, even in the face of our own self-condemnation and incredulous minds, the hope of glory refuses to be silenced. Somewhere deep inside us we have a universal and undeniable thirst and a nagging sense of purpose that defies even our own doubts. But only Jesus Christ has the capacity to break into the darkness of our unbelief and turn the lights on. In him, the hope of glory finds its mark, and life takes on new dimensions of meaning.

PART ONE

The Glory of God

2

GLORY OF GOD IN HUMAN FLESH

Who is Jesus, Really?

Jesus once asked his disciples who people were saying that he was. They replied, saying,

"Some say John the Baptist; others say Elijah; and still others, Jeremiah or one of the prophets."

"But what about you?" he asked. "Who do you say that I am?"

Simon Peter answered, "You are the Messiah, the Son of the living God" (Matthew 16: 13-16).

If I were to loosely translate what Peter was saying it would look something like this,

"I know who you are! You're the one we Jews have been waiting for all these years; the one who will fulfil all the promises made to Abraham — you're the Messiah! Which means: *you're* the Son of God!"

Amazingly, Peter had seen something which is impossible for any human being to see without the self-revelation of God, and Jesus immediately realized the enormous transformation in Simon Peter's perception: "Blessed are you, Simon son of Jonah, for this was not revealed to you by flesh and blood, but by my Father in heaven" (Matthew 16: 17).

But there's even more going on here. What Peter would've previously understood by the term 'Son of God' was very different from what he was now seeing in the person who stood in front of him. Peter — like any full-blooded Jew in his day — almost certainly had an image of the "Son of God" as a warrior king striding into town with unstoppable power, armies of angels at his command, his sword of vengeance dark with the blood of Israel's enemies, who would then establish the everlasting physical kingdom of God in Jerusalem.

This revelation of the true identity of Jesus was completely redefining the meaning of "Son of God." Peter was beginning to see things with new eyes; to see what would've been impossible to see without God making it see-able. As Jesus put it elsewhere, "No one knows the Son except the Father, and no one knows the Father except the Son and those to whom the Son chooses to reveal him" (Matthew 11: 27).

Jesus went on and explained to Peter that it would be on this otherwise inconceivable revelation that the Church would ultimately be built and stand strong through the ages. So wonderful would this revelation be that nothing and no one would be able to restrain it: not even death (Matthew 16: 18). As far as Jesus is concerned, the revelation of his true identity as the Son of God is at the very heart of the gospel.

So what's so significant about Jesus being the Son of God? Don't we already know that? As a matter of pure routine fact, the answer is, 'yes,' but like Peter, we often struggle to know just what that fact really means.

Forgotten Truth

I once heard a fisherman refer to someone as "a bream-less marlin-catcher." Bream are the most common and easy-to-catch fish on the east coast of Australia and just about everyone who has ever dangled a line there has caught plenty of them. Later they might go on to catch other fish such as salmon or tailor. Later still, they may even advance to more difficult-to-catch fish such as trout or tuna. Eventually, given enough time, money and skill, they might even catch the greatest prize of the angling world: a marlin. In more recent times, however, people with a pile of money can easily afford to go on a game fishing charter and catch a marlin on their very first outing, never really appreciating the finer points of angling or seamanship for themselves.

I sometimes think we twenty-first century Christians who have had 2000 years of tradition and theology simply handed to us could be 'bream-less marlin-catchers' too. We can easily miss the significance of things for which our predecessors bled and died. I believe the meaning and significance of Jesus as the 'Son of God' is one of those things. The truth about who Jesus Christ really is remains the single most essential element of our lives and faith — whether we acknowledge it or not.

Could a Man Really be God?

At first glance, Jesus could easily be passed over as just another prophet or great teacher. Who could have suspected that Jesus was in fact divine — the Son of God? He is, after all, just a human being, but there's more to this man than meets the eye. Even the disciples were often puzzled by Christ and left guessing about his real identity.

For instance, when Jesus calmed the wind and the waves with a single command, they were utterly astonished and asked, "Who is this man?"(Luke 8: 25). Or when the disciples heard Jesus pray they were similarly amazed pleading, "Teach us to pray" (Luke 11: 1). It was as if they were saying, "We want to pray like you do. We thought we were praying well enough until we heard you. That was real prayer," or the time Peter — a full-time professional fisherman — decided to humour Jesus after he told him to put down his nets in the wrong place and at the wrong time of day — yet ended up catching a huge haul of fish (Luke 5: 1-11).

I believe the thing the disciples were seeing, which marked Jesus as unique among human beings, was simply the way he carried himself in the world. He was always perfectly at ease with everyone he met, no matter who they were. But even more amazing was the way he spoke comfortably and directly with God and addressed him typically as "Father." For a Jew to address God as 'Father' in an intimate or familiar way was considered a serious blasphemy. On one occasion, after Jesus declared "I and the Father are one," some of his hearers were intent on lynching him on the spot and accused him of blasphemy "because you, a *mere man*, claim to be God"

(John 10: 30-32). This was the real reason the elders of Israel ultimately condemned him to death (Matthew 26: 64-67).

Not that you could blame the Jews for thinking this way: who could have imagined that the all-powerful maker of heaven and earth would even consider being confined to the lowly status of a human being? The irony caught everyone by surprise. It's certainly not the kind of 'glory' the messiah-watchers were waiting for. But, as is often the case, the glory of God is revealed where it's most concealed.

God becoming a human being — what theologians call the *incarnation* — really is an incredible and astonishing event. Yet two thousand years on we have come to take it all for granted.

Before Creation

The disciples of Jesus weren't taking these things for granted, that's for sure. For them, the incarnation was world-changing. Finally the lid had been lifted on who God really is, and what the Kingdom of God is really all about. Post Pentecost they came to fully realize the vital significance of who Jesus is and what that would mean for the whole world.

Of all the disciples, John seems to have understood the implications most deeply. He begins his account of the Gospel by going right back to before creation. "In the beginning was the Word, and the Word was with God, and the Word was God. He was with God in the beginning" (John 1: 1). This is the first word of the Gospel right here. It precedes everything — even creation.

When John writes "the Word was *with* God" he means far more than simply being in the same neighbourhood. He is writing of an ongoing and face-to-face relationship. This means that before anything was created, God wasn't sitting around bored and lonely in a cold empty void. Far from it! Love, joy, conversation, friendship and laughter preceded and always existed before creation. Jesus said as much when he prayed to the Father just before his crucifixion, "And now, Father, glorify me in your presence with the glory I had with you before the world began" (John 17: 5). I'd like to suggest this 'with-ness' — the connection, life and love that Jesus the Son has in relationship with the Father — *is* the glory he's talking about here, and it's this magnificent union that ultimately defines him as Son.

But here's the thing: this 'with-ness' that Jesus has enjoyed for eternity with the Father has now been earthed and revealed as the Son of God becomes a human being. Now the glory of God — the essential character and nature of the Trinity — is on full and accessible display in the humanity of Jesus Christ. As John has it a few verses later, "We have seen his glory, the glory of the one and only Son, who came from the Father, full of grace and truth" (John 1: 14). I find many people are confused by the idea of the Trinity and the concept of the 'three-being-one,' but it has nothing to do with arithmetic. It's all about the utter oneness of heart, mind and purpose, shared between the Father, Son and Holy Spirit; and it's *this* oneness that Jesus embodies which constitutes his glory.

More than words

But what does John mean when he says that Jesus is the Word of God? To answer this question it is necessary to first understand what this usage of 'Word'' actually means. What, after all, is a word?

A word is perhaps best understood as the gathered and arranged rationale of a certain body of knowledge, which is then declared and transferred from one person to another. A word is a means of conveying a thought, or an intention, or a will from one to another. For instance the written words you are reading right now convey my thoughts to you to some degree. You are beginning to know me — just a little — through these words. But the problem with written words is that they are indirect and second-hand. If, on the other hand, I were to ring you on the phone and engage you in conversation, my spoken words would convey even more of myself to you. The tone of my voice, my accent and emotions would all say something more about me. Best of all, would be if I were to meet you face-to-face: then my whole body and being would become a 'word.'

Apparently I cannot verbally hide things from my wife — not successfully anyway. She knows me so well that no matter what I *say*, the real truth is all too evident in my body language. The subtle nuances of my voice, the position of my eyebrows and the way I sit, all conspire to send a 'word' that reveals my innermost thoughts.

This is precisely what John means when he writes, "The Word became flesh and made his dwelling among us" (John 1: 14). What a remarkable statement. Jesus is more than a messenger: he *is* the Message. He's not merely the teller of a word *from* God: he *is* God! All other human words — religious, philosophical and cultural — are eclipsed by *the* Word. For the Word we see in Jesus is a revelation of the ultimate truth: the inner being and nature of God. In him we see God *fully* glorified.

'I will Dwell with You'

This means Jesus didn't just come and dwell among us merely to deliver a message to us. His dwelling among us is actually what it's all about — his dwelling *is* the message he came to give us. Just as the Son has always dwelled with the Father, now he has come to share the nature and magnificence of their mutual 'dwelling' with us, so that we might "become children of God" (John 1: 12). This is another way of saying that we will ultimately come to dwell with God and know the very same 'with-ness' that Jesus has always known and experienced with the Father. As Baxter Kruger has it:

> Before creation, it was decided that the Son would cross every chasm between the triune God and humanity and establish a real and abiding union with us. Jesus was predestined to be the mediator, the One in and through whom the very life of the triune God would enter human existence, and human existence would be lifted up to share in the trinitarian life.[iv]

God didn't reveal his glory in the incarnation just so we might admire it. His intention was for us to participate in it!

Restrained Truth

Yet most often when I hear preaching about the incarnation — if at all — it's nearly always about how Jesus came to dwell among us so that he could redeem us. While I do believe that notion is perfectly sound and true, we must also go on to say God redeems us for himself, so we can dwell with him: after all atonement is really all about *at-one-ment*.

This determination in the heart of God is first mentioned in the story of the Exodus when God declared to Moses that the Israelites were to be delivered up out of Egypt "so that I might dwell among them" (Exodus 29: 46). The goal of the Exodus wasn't to merely save Israel from Egypt, but to liberate them so that they could dwell freely with God. The Exodus story is the Old Testament forerunner to the New Testament Gospel. It's a primer for the ultimate purpose of salvation that Jesus Christ brings to his people — and the plan hasn't changed. The grand purpose of the incarnation and the meaning of salvation is this: God dwelling with us and us with God.

Yet somewhere in history we seem to have largely forgotten this vital truth.

I once dropped into my local Christian bookshop specifically to purchase a two-part commentary on the epistle to the Romans. I was amazed to discover there were over a dozen copies of the second volume gathering dust on the shelves while the first volume was sold out. I didn't understand at first.

Then it dawned on me.

The first half of Romans is all about the means and process of salvation while the second is mostly about the ultimate purpose of salvation — the glorification of creation, restoration of Israel, the conclusion of the covenants and so on. It seems to me that ever since the reformation — despite its necessary and remedial effect — we've become so fixated with 'getting saved' we've overlooked the end goal salvation serves: that we would come to know the God that Jesus knows as Father, so that we too would know the Father and therefore be ready to take our place in the restoration of creation.

The incarnation was vital for salvation — granted — but that wasn't the only reason that Jesus came in the flesh. Jesus came to share the glory of his oneness with the Father with us. The Apostle Paul states it plainly in his second epistle to the Thessalonians:

> God chose you as firsfruits to be saved through the sanctifying work of the Spirit and through belief in the truth. He called you to this through our gospel, *that you might share in the glory of our Lord Jesus Christ.*
>
> — 2 Thessalonians 2: 13-14

The grand plan of the incarnation includes, not only salvation from sin, but sharing in the glory of Christ.

Only Jesus is capable of doing this because he alone is the unique Son of the Father.

3

GLORY OF THE FATHER AND THE SON

Only Jesus Knows the Father

I remember watching a documentary about the life and times of the once President of the United States, John F. Kennedy. It included a short piece of film showing JFK stepping from an aeroplane onto the tarmac, surrounded by the top brass of the armed forces and high ranking government officials with their peaked hats, uniforms and all the trappings of military might. Suddenly, from the gathered crowd of onlookers, a small boy dashed across the tarmac and leapt into the arms of the President. The boy, of course, was his son.

It would be hard to imagine anyone else having the liberty or temerity to do likewise. If they had, I expect they would have been wrestled to the ground by the secret service — or worse. Doubtless some of these men worked with the president day-in and day-out and could say they *knew* him very well. Some of them were probably even his friends. But for all their familiarity, none of them knew what the little boy knew.

Something like this is true about Jesus Christ and the Father. No matter how well any prophet or theologian claims to know God, only Jesus knows God as Father. The most significant thing we can say about Jesus Christ is that he is the Son of God. Only Jesus can make the essential character and nature of the Father truly known. The incarnation of the Son of God was ultimately to glorify the Father.

It's simply not enough to say Jesus came to die for our sins, or to heal the sick, or teach us the truth. The main thing Jesus came to do was make God known as Father. How, then, does Jesus reveal the Father?

Mutual glorification

When I unwittingly became a birdwatcher, I soon discovered there was more to it than I initially realized. The more I appreciated and understood the complexities of bird-life, the more I appreciated the habitats they called home. Each species requires a very specific and distinct set of environmental conditions in order to survive. The more I become fascinated with birds, the more I found myself becoming fascinated with trees and rocks, rivers and grass. In fact, it isn't possible to really grow in knowledge of birds without simultaneously growing in knowledge of the environment: they are inherently linked.

In a much more profound way, if we come to really know Jesus as the Son of God, we will inevitably come to know the

Father as well. Indeed it's impossible to know one without the other because we discover who Jesus really is by seeing the way he relates to his Father. To really *know* Jesus is to also *know* the Father. As Jesus put it, "Anyone who has seen me has seen the Father" (John 14: 9).

Relational Identity

Similarly to Jesus' identity being found in the Father, it's the significant relationships in our lives that define us more than where we live or what we do. I once wrote a random list of all the roles that somehow shape my identity and it ended up looking something like this: "I'm a friend, a pastor, an artist, a father, a preacher, a husband, an angler, a son, an Australian, a brother." Then I rearranged the list in descending order of importance. As you might expect the top half of the list was all about my closest relationships while the things I do were relegated to the bottom of the list. Our identity is mostly defined by those we love and not so much by other categories such as our work, hobbies, or nationality.

Similarly, God is most potently revealed in relational terms and not by so-called 'divine attributes' such as omnipotence, omnipresence, and omniscience. Knowing that God is all powerful is one thing, but to know God is love, is entirely another. Any rank-and-file prophet can tell you "God is great" but only the Son can *show* us the Father. As the great early church theologian Athanasius put it, "It is more devout and more precise to know God as Father through Jesus the Son than to know God as creator through the things he has made."ᵛ

A Glorious Son reveals a Glorious Father

Shortly before the crucifixion, Jesus explained relational identity to his disciples: "Now the Son of Man [Jesus Christ] is glorified and God is glorified in Him" (John 13: 31). Peterson's translation of this, and the following verse, captures it beautifully: "Now the Son of Man is seen for who he is, and God is seen for who he is in him. The moment God is seen in him, God's glory will be on display. In glorifying him, he himself is glorified — glory all around!"[vi] So the Son brings glory to the Father by simply *being* the Son. Put in other words: and the sort of father the Father is, is seen in the sort of son the Son is.

This may seem a little esoteric at first, but this same principle is in action all around us. Walking in my local neighbourhood recently, I couldn't help noticing that some of the gardens were spectacular, filled with colour and life. As the gardener 'glorifies' the garden, the garden 'glorifies' the gardener. The corollary is true too. My garden, for instance, does little to glorify *its* gardener (stupid garden!).

This can all be applied in principle to marriage, parenthood, government, business, education and more besides. The way a government, for example, treats its people will determine how the people with ultimately 'glorify' their government in the long-term. We operate this way because everything in creation is built upon the nature of the original relationships between the Father, Son and Holy Spirit.

So, the truth about who God really is, and what he's really like, is best seen in the way the Father and the Son relate to and love one another in the Holy Spirit, and the incarnation of the Son is the way God has chosen to make this relationship known to us. It's both that simple, and yet that profound.

What Sort of son is the Son?

Many people would agree that Jesus Christ is the most extraordinary human being who ever lived, but it wasn't just the spectacular moments and miracles that set Jesus apart. He was extraordinary in the ordinary as well. Indeed, some of the most remarkable displays of glory are seen in the most unremarkable ways.

Take, for instance, this amazing sentence in the Gospel of John, "Jesus knew that the Father had put all things under his power, and that he had come from God and was returning to God; *so* he got up from the meal, took off his outer clothing, and wrapped a towel around his waist" (John 13: 3-4). The story goes on to explain how Jesus then washed his disciples' feet — normally the job of a low-paid servant or slave.

There's a whole world of things going on in this story.

For starters I cannot think of a single person in history who 'knowing that everything was under their power' would take on the role of a lowly servant. What sort of person would do this? The answer, of course, is someone like Jesus: someone who is so secure and so sure of the Father's love that he could be trusted with great power.

There's something more here that could easily be overlooked. According to John, in doing this Jesus was practically demonstrating the fullness of his love (John 13: 1): he was pointing to the cross in this act of foot washing as a foreshadowing of the ultimate act of service. It was a forerunner to the main event. Later Jesus explained, "As the

Father has loved me, so have I loved you" (John 15: 9). Can you see what is going on here? Jesus is demonstrating to his disciples the kind of love he is used to experiencing from the Father. *The way the Son loves us is the same way the Father loves the Son.* The Son serves as he is served by the Father, loves as he is loved by the Father, and gives as he is given to by the Father.

For whatever reason, most people I have talked with have an image of the Father as the 'boss-God,' while the Son is a kind of subordinate 'servant-God.' But, if the words of Jesus are to be taken seriously, then we must adjust our view of the Father to fall in line with the nature of the love we see flowing from the Son. The Father has been 'washing the feet' of the Son for eternity. This is to say, the Father has been showing the Son the full extent of his love throughout eternity in continuous, humble, self-giving action. Little wonder, then, that the Son is the kind of Son he is — secure and strong, yet gentle and meek.

The Son Knows he is Loved

With this in view, Jesus never felt abandoned, threatened or anxious, and it never crossed Jesus' mind to act independently of the Father (John 5: 19, 16: 32). The way Jesus speaks and the things he does are precisely as the Father speaks and acts, because the Father and the Son are of one mind and one purpose about *everything*.

So sure was Jesus of the Father's love he was able to openly declare, "For the Father loves the Son and shows him all he does" (John 5: 20). Jesus went on to explain how the Father trusts the Son with everything he is doing — even to the giving of life and ultimate judgement. In Jesus' own words, "the Father judges no one, but has entrusted all judgement to the Son, *that all may honor the Son as they honor the Father*" (John 5: 22-23). This means the Father is holding nothing back from the Son and there's no hint of the Father 'bossing' the Son around. Instead, we see the Son has an equal share of the authority and the honor of the Father.

The Son loves the Father

The most obvious way Jesus responds to the love of the Father is in his joyful obedience to the will of the Father. In Jesus' own words, "I love the Father and do exactly what my Father has commanded me" (John 14: 31). At first glance this may seem to be contrary with the claims of the previous paragraphs. Let's take a closer look at what's really going on here.

Obedience is not a word we generally see in a positive light. Doubtless this is because we rarely (if ever) see a pure-hearted demonstration of the kind of obedience mentioned here. The obedience we are most familiar with is what I like to call 'expedient obedience.' This kind of 'obedience' is usually little more than dutiful compliance with the rules as a means of keeping out of trouble, or in the 'good books,' with authority. Keeping to the speed limit merely to avoid getting a speeding ticket is an example of 'expedient obedience.' But the 'obedience' of the Son is entirely different to this.

For Jesus, obedience is an act of love. It's his joyful agreement with the Father. He's so certain of his Father's goodwill and so secure in his love that he gladly embraces the commands of his Father and delights in doing his will.

This kind of sonly obedience is worlds away from slavish subordination.

Slaving and Sonning

Some years ago, I was snorkelling on a coral reef, where the black and white Banded Sea-snake is commonly encountered. Unlike their terrestrial cousins, sea-snakes are essentially docile and relatively harmless,[vii] so when I came across a sea-snake with its head down a hole in the sand I thought it would be safe to gently pick up the tail section. What I thought was a Banded Sea-snake actually turned out to be a Banded Eel instead. It looked almost exactly the same as the snake but the eel has none of its counterpart's docile characteristics. The eel immediately withdrew its head from the hole and attacked me with demon fury. I backed away as fast as I could, but the eel kept coming. It took several long anxious moments and a couple of well-placed kicks to dissuade the eel from taking a chunk out of me.

On the surface, slaving may look a lot like genuine obedience, but ultimately it's self-preserving expedience. They're two completely different species.

Do you remember the parable of the prodigal son? The parable is, of course, broader than its popular title would suggest. It's really a story about a *father* and his *two* sons. The older brother of the prodigal son did not leave the family farm but stayed home working for the father while his younger brother was off squandering his inheritance on wild living. When the younger son came home, the father was so overjoyed he threw a huge party to celebrate. The older son was indignant and complained to the father saying, "Look! All these years I have been *slaving* for you and never disobeyed your orders" (Luke 15: 29). But sons are not meant to slave.

Notice what the father says to the son in response: "My son, you are always with me and everything I have is yours" (Luke 15: 31). The father and the son have an equal share in the family estate; they have a mutuality of honor and privilege. The son isn't diminished by serving his father. On the contrary: he's enlarging their mutual wealth. He didn't see that everything that belonged to the father also belonged to him: he forgot who he was and acted like a slave instead. Not so with Jesus the true Son. He happily obeys the Father and shares in the Father's delight and goodness. The obedience of Jesus is a participation in a continuous mutuality of giving and receiving; of love responding to love.

Mutual Glory

Take, for instance, the story at the beginning of the fourth chapter of John where we find Jesus, hungry and thirsty, sitting at Jacob's well while his disciples have headed into town to buy food. (John 4: 4-7). While they're away, Jesus falls into a protracted and interesting conversation with a Samaritan woman who'd come to the well to draw water. The woman is transformed by her encounter with Jesus and eventually rushes back to town to tell everybody about him (John 4: 28-30). By this time the disciples have returned and urge Jesus to eat some food, to which Jesus replies, "I have food to eat that you know nothing about." The disciples are mystified. Where did he get food, they wonder? Jesus explained, "My food is to do the will of him who sent me and to finish his work" (John 4: 32-34). Here we see Jesus, far from being diminished by his service, he is enlarged by it. It's the joy and the privilege of the Son to do the will of the Father.

Even more profoundly, in the second chapter of his letter to the Philippians Paul beautifully captures the paradoxical nature of Christ's humility and resulting glorification:

> And being found in appearance as a man, he humbled himself by becoming obedient to death — even death on a cross! Therefore God exalted him to the highest place and gave him the name that is above every name, that at the name of Jesus every knee should bow, in heaven and on earth, and every tongue acknowledge that Jesus Christ is Lord, *to the glory of God the Father*.
>
> — Philippians 2: 8-11

As Jesus willingly and freely submits himself to death on a cross in open agreement with the Father, the true nature of his sonship is thoroughly and powerfully displayed. Then, as the Son is glorified, he simultaneously reveals the glory of the Father. In the humility of the crucifixion the true nature of the Father's self-giving, other-centred love is perfectly unveiled by the Son. So, even though the Father and the Son have different roles, they have equal glory.

This is the supreme revelation of the true nature of God, because here we discover God in profoundly relational terms. For the more the Father loves and serves the Son, the more the Son is enriched and secured, which in turn strengthens the Son in his capacity and desire to love and serve the Father. This is precisely what Jesus prayed shortly before the crucifixion: "Father, the hour has come. Glorify your Son, that your Son may glorify you" (John 17: 1). In effect, Jesus was praying, 'Father, please *father* me, so that I in turn may *son* you.'

Paradoxically, as the Father and the Son give themselves to the other and mutually indwell one another, the more their unique characteristics are defined. Rather than being absorbed into one another and losing their distinct 'colours' in a homogenised blend, their 'colours' are actually intensified by their oneness. The vivid hues of the Father are luminously accentuated by the exquisite tints of the Son, and vice-versa.

It's impossible to comprehend the unlimited depths of relationship and connection between the Father and the Son. Their oneness is unspeakably infinite and immeasurable. Yet somehow the fullness of their mutual indwelling is mysteriously revealed in the humanity of Jesus Christ.

Overflowing Glory

This all leads us to yet another magnificent quality in the nature of the Father-Son relationship: the fullness of their inward connection is reflected by their outward intention. Creation and salvation are, therefore, the deliberate outflow of their inflow.

So free and full is the love shared between the Father, Son and Holy Spirit (by the way, we will talk a whole lot more about the Holy Spirit a little later) that it intentionally and freely spills outward to include humanity as well. In Jesus' words, "Now a slave has no permanent place in the family, but a son belongs to it forever. So if the Son sets you free, you shall be free indeed" (John 8: 35-36). I believe Jesus is saying, "If you would only let me free you from slavery to know the liberty of *my* sonship, then you would finally know what it means to be truly, permanently and wonderfully free in the family of God."

And that is precisely what Jesus *wants* us to know.

4

GLORY ALL AROUND

The Goal of Salvation

I used to live in the small city of Darwin in the tropical north of Australia — happily for me, one of the best places in the world for bird-watching. The northern shores of Australia are the eventual destination of millions of migrant wading birds that fly all the way from Siberia to escape the Northern Hemisphere winter. Oddly enough the sewage treatment works just outside Darwin is *the* premier place to see the rarest of these sojourners. Access to the sewage works is therefore a much coveted privilege for keen bird-watchers. As a member of the local club however I was fortunate enough to have a key. I've never fully understood the need for sewage pits — of all places — to be locked up and secured with high barbed-wire fences; suffice to say these particular pits were uncommonly well guarded.

One morning a friend and I met at the gates of the treatment works in the pre-dawn gloom to do a bit of birding. Just as we entered the compound we discovered an unfortunate fruit-bat tangled in the barbed-wire of the fence. To make matters worse, sitting either side of the fruit-bat were several Black Kites, a kind of carrion-eating bird as close to a vulture as Australia can produce. Doubtless they were waiting for the sun to rise, and the eventual death of the hapless bat.

The bat's plaintive cries stirred our sympathies and we decided to save it from such a miserable end. This was not as easy as it sounds. Fruit bats, it must be understood, are not like ordinary bats. They can have a wingspan up to one and a half metres and a bad temper to match. Nevertheless, we somehow managed to clamber up the fence and disentangle the bat, all the while avoiding its needle sharp teeth and the barbed-wire. After several fretful minutes we succeeded in extracting the bat from the fence and triumphantly held it spreadeagled between us. Then in the glow of a beautiful tropical dawn, we launched it into the breeze and watched it gracefully soar toward freedom and away from the malevolence of the Black Kites.

Sadly, the bat was so exhausted by its nocturnal ordeal that it began to lose altitude before spiralling out of control into the middle of a sewage pit. Out of the frying pan and into the fire, so to speak. Undeterred however, we fished the sodden creature from the sewage and towelled it off before coming up with a better plan — one we really ought to have executed in the first place. Just outside the compound stood a dense forest of mangrove trees, and in the trees, a camp of fruit bats numbering in the thousands. We released the bat at the base of a mangrove tree and it quickly scurried up to the canopy where it re-joined its extended family.

This entire episode is etched into my mind as an allegory of salvation. Salvation is not just about what we are saved *from* – sin and death – it's what we are saved *into* that really counts.

Glorious Humanity

Being saved from sin and death *is* good news, clearly, but *the* Good News is even better news than that. Just like the fruit-bat, our salvation is ultimately about being restored to our proper place in relationship to God, to one another, and to the rest of creation. It's all about being what we were originally created to be.

The early church theologian Irenaeus once wrote, "The glory of God is a man fully alive, and the life of man is to behold God."[viii] I believe Irenaeus has perfectly captured in one sentence what salvation is all about. But the only person who fits the description of "a man fully alive" is Jesus Christ, and he's also the only person who has a proper vision of God. There can be no such thing as a man or woman 'fully alive' apart from Christ.

Jesus not only shows us who God really is: he also gives us a grand re-vision of true humanity. Although he was just like us with all the frailties and limitations of our humanity, he was also unlike anyone who had ever lived before. This is not to say that Jesus was super-human, rather he was *fully* human. A magnificent, fully alive, glorious human being.

Sharing the Glory Around

Jesus is the tangible embodiment of the love of God. Jesus didn't enter human life just to give us a wonderful example to copy, or a standard to live up to: he came to share his life and his vision of God with us.

Do you remember the account of Jesus speaking with Mary Magdalene in the garden after the resurrection? He said to her, "tell them, I am ascending to my Father and *your* Father, to my God and *your* God" (John 20: 17). The incarnation is all about including us in the circle of love that has always existed between the Father, Son and Holy Spirit. God *wants* us to share in the glory of their oneness.

Incarnation wasn't a temporary job for Jesus either. He didn't just slum it for thirty odd years in a 'man suit' before re-entering heavenly glory. He became human *forever*, whilst remaining wholly divine. The glory of divine life has been irrevocably and permanently joined to human life in the humanity of Jesus Christ. Think of it: right now, in the circle of love shared between the Trinity, is a real flesh-and-blood human being just like you or me. In astounding humility, Jesus Christ has forged a union between divine and human life on behalf of all humanity. The implications are stunning, not least of all for our understanding of the ultimate goal of salvation. It's not just what we are saved from, but what we are saved into that really counts.

Eternal Life

It would be safe to say that John 3: 16 is one of the best known and most quoted verses in the Bible when it comes to talking about salvation: "For God so loved the world that he gave his one and only Son, that whoever believes in him shall not perish but have eternal life." But what exactly is eternal life? Jesus defined it this way, "Now this is eternal life: that they may know you, the only true God, and Jesus Christ, whom you have sent" (John 17: 3). Eternal life is not about 'heaven' as a place we go to so much as it's about being caught up into the relationship between the Father and Son. It's having a share in the face-to-face communion, oneness and joy that Jesus has with his Father in the Holy Spirit.

When our children were little, they loved nothing more than to crawl into bed and fall asleep in the space between Catherine and me. Normally this was all well and good, but on a hot summer night the last thing we needed was another hot little body radiating heat between us. Instinctively we would edge our way to the furthest extremities of the mattress in an attempt to remain cool. Just as instinctively, our children would lie diagonally stretched out across the space between us with a toe prodding a knee on one side and an index finger jabbed into a shoulder (or an eye) on the other. They just needed to know we were both still there. It was a beautiful albeit irritating thing. Similarly I believe the 'space' between the Father and Son is instinctively where we all long to be. Jesus defines it as 'eternal life.'

This does not mean that we lose our humanity and take on divinity: on the contrary, we become more truly and magnificently human through our union with God. Just as the distinctions of the Father and Son are defined by their oneness, so too the closer we are drawn into the eternal life of God, the more human we become.

That's the point of salvation.

It's not enough or even accurate to say that Jesus came to die on a cross for the forgiveness of our sins so that we will 'go to heaven' when we die. Redemption and forgiveness are not ends in themselves so much as the means to an end — that we would come to know the Father and share in the relationship that Jesus has with the Father. The final goal is our full and magnificent glorification. It's finding our place in the life and love shared between the Father and the Son, our place in the family of God.

A Glorious Prayer

Jesus himself clearly declared these very things in his astonishing prayer recorded in the seventeenth chapter of John. The implications of this prayer are almost too wonderful to imagine; just look at these amazing words:

> My prayer is not for them alone. I pray also for those who will believe in me through their message, that all of them may be one, Father, just as you are in me and I am in you. May they also be in us so the world may believe that you have sent me. *I have given them the glory that you gave me,* that they may be one as we are one — I in them and you in me — so that they may be brought to complete unity. Then the world will know that you have sent me and *have loved them even as you have loved me.* Father, I want those you have given to me to be with me where I am, and to see my glory, the glory you have given me because you loved me before the creation of the world. Righteous Father, though the world does not know you, I know you, and they know that you have sent me. I have made you known to them,

and will continue to make you known in order that the love you have
for me may be in them and that I myself may be in them.

— John 17: 20-26

I don't even know where to start with this! Could these words really be true? Was Jesus seriously saying that we are loved in exactly the same way and to the same degree that he is loved? That his glory would be given to us? That *he* himself would be *in* us?

Too Good to be True?

It's a really interesting thing to watch the reaction of most people when I read this passage out in public. I have made a particular point of closely observing how all kinds of people, in all kinds of places, respond to these words. Most people look down and begin to lose interest. This is odd, given that these words must be among the most beautiful and most significant ever spoken by anyone, anywhere, ever. When I ask people what their thoughts are after hearing "I have made you known to them, and will continue to make you known in order that the love you have for me may be in them and that I myself may be in them" the response is usually one of incredulity.

Why is this so? The answer, I believe, is very simple: it seems too good to be true! But every now and then the truth somehow sneaks past our defences and startles us. I well remember reading this prayer and actually *seeing* the words for the first time. Something like a depth-charge detonated deep in my soul and the shock waves are still reverberating to this day. I could hardly believe what I was reading. Yet, there it was, all plainly laid out in black and white, and in the Bible no less, the very words of Jesus in prayer. For days, and then months after, I remember being in a wonderful state of bliss as I realized the implications of these words.

Over the years I've talked with dozens of people who have had similar reactions as the import of this prayer has unexpectedly struck them. Take, for instance, this account sent by a friend a few years ago after realizing the truth of these things:

> Do you have any books I could read that specifically expand on the fact that the Father loves me as much as he loves Jesus? I *so* hope it's true but it still seems *too* huge. I don't want to relax in it just in case I find out it's not true — not that I don't believe you; I just find it hard to believe *it*. Loving me the way I thought he did was enough but if this really sinks in it will change my whole life and perspective and *everything*. I couldn't sleep on Saturday night. I didn't want to lose that feeling of the enormity of his love even if I eventually find out it's not true, I just wanted to hold onto it (and still do) for a bit longer. I don't want to tell too many people in case they theologise some clever spiel to shrink God's love for me. So let me get this straight: he loves me as much as he loves himself? [sic] Or have I gone too far? Looking forward to hearing from you before I go nuts.... or before somebody bursts my bubble.

Usually we don't need somebody else to 'burst the bubble' for us. We manage to do that for ourselves: our incredulity causes the gospel to ricochet right off our hearts.

I once heard the tragic story of a man who simply couldn't form a single lasting relationship with anyone. It didn't take long to discover why. When he was a small boy he was standing on the back of a tray-top truck when his father held out his arms and said to him, "Jump into my arms son." He jumped. His father took a step back and let the boy fall heavily and painfully to the ground. His father looked down at his son and jabbing his index finger into the boy's face he said, "That was to teach you to never trust anyone." Unsurprisingly, he never did.

Sadly we have all experienced — to lesser or greater degrees — this same kind of disillusionment. Over time we gradually let the icy fingers of cynicism strangle the life out of our hopes and faith as we succumb to the bitter numbness of unbelief.

Truth is Better than Fiction

But just for fun let's imagine that Jesus really *meant* what he said when he prayed for "those who will believe in me through their message," and let's assume that Jesus sometimes gets a positive answer to his prayers. Then, just maybe, it might actually be possible that we really are loved by God. Not just accepted; not just forgiven; but deeply, magnificently and thoroughly loved — even liked! Loved by the Father in exactly the same way and degree the Father loves the Son.

"But I'm so unworthy and unlovable," I hear you say. No argument from me. I can well believe it. But that's the point! That's what salvation is all about. This is not a relationship we have manufactured or forged our way into. We can't earn it or make it happen; we can only receive it as a gift. We can only let God love us.[ix]

The most important relationship you have is not *your* relationship with God. The most important relationship *you have* is the relationship *Jesus has* with the Father.ˣ Our so-called relationship with God is not what counts. Rather, it is sharing in the relationship the Son has with the Father. This is our glorification: relating to the Father as true children; sharing in the inheritance of the elder brother Jesus; and enjoying fellowship with the Holy Spirit. What could be better than that?

How can we possibly encounter this truth in a real and living way? Like the man who cried out to Jesus when he desperately needed help, "I do believe; help me overcome my unbelief!" (Mark 9: 24), there is one who will help us. We are not left to our own devices or ingenuity in order to access the mystery of these truths. In the next chapter we will begin to discover the role of the Holy Spirit in sharing the glory around.

5

GLORY OF THE HOLY SPIRIT

Real Truth

I talked with a woman some time ago who wanted to find out the truth about Jesus for herself by travelling to Israel. She regaled me with a story of her journey to Jerusalem where she visited the supposed site of the crucifixion: she had hoped for a mystical encounter or an epiphany of some sort on the hallowed ground of Christ's vicarious death. Instead, somebody tried to sell her a tee-shirt and she ended up in a heated argument with the would-be vendor. The problem was simply that she was two thousand years too late.

Indeed, we're all two thousand years too late.

But would it really make a difference if we had actually been in Jerusalem two thousand years ago? How many times have you heard people say, "If only I had been there when

Jesus walked the streets of Jerusalem and saw the miracles he did and heard the words he said — then I would *really* believe"? Maybe: maybe not. There were plenty of people who *did* witness the miracles and hear Jesus teach; and watched him die; and even saw him raised to life — and yet they still did not believe. Seeing, it turns out, is not necessarily believing.

It has always intrigued me how the Pharisees reacted to the story of the resurrection of Lazarus in John 11: 38-53. Under any circumstances the raising of a man who was previously a rotting corpse is fairly compelling evidence that Jesus Christ really was who he claimed to be. Doubtless the news of this event spread far and wide, and its veracity could be easily confirmed by unbiased witnesses. The Pharisees did not call into question the facts of the case. What is remarkable however, is that they remained obstinate in the face of the report and even plotted to have Jesus and Lazarus murdered.

Later still, when these same men heard the impartial report of the guards who were assigned to keep watch over the tomb of Jesus, they once again brushed off the implications of the event and bribed the guards to tell everyone that the disciples of Christ had come in the night to steal away his body (Matthew 28: 11-15). Interestingly, this same rumour is still very much in circulation today. The guards must have been paid handsomely, given that their rumour has been so particularly effective, and given the amazing story that they were forced to suppress. Imagine it: angels, earthquakes, dead-man-walking — it had everything! Yet they agreed to keep their mouths shut!

Impossible Possibility

Even the disciples struggled to have faith, despite all the things they witnessed first-hand. What hope, then, is there for us who have *not* walked the streets of Jerusalem with Jesus or witnessed his death and resurrection? Yet Jesus said, "blessed are those who have not seen and yet have believed" (John 20: 29). How is this belief possible?

The simple answer is: the Holy Spirit. Jesus explained to his disciples that when the Spirit came he would guide them "into all the truth" (John 16: 13). Jesus was not saying that the Spirit would guide them into all the facts or all the theology. By 'truth,' Jesus was meaning "all the reality." The Holy Spirit does more than simply take us up to the truth as an objective fact — he leads us *into* the truth in such a way that it indwells and penetrates our entire being.

For instance there is a world of difference between knowing the doctrine of forgiveness of sin and experiencing the dynamic truth of the forgiveness of sin. Being brought up in a strong Christian home I was well aware of the doctrine of forgiveness but had never really experienced forgiveness. I knew the scriptures well enough and could quote chapter and verse on most key subjects but failed to make any real connection between the doctrine I knew *about* God and the *God* the doctrine was about. As a youth I regularly attended every church meeting, youth activity, and evangelistic rally, and would often times respond to 'altar calls' in various states of contrition seeking peace with God.

Nothing ever happened.

Then, for no particular reason, the truth of forgiveness was opened to me in a powerful, palpable way. I was listening to a preacher as he expounded the first three verses of the fifth chapter of Romans when it happened. It was just another ordinary day, in an ordinary little church hall, in an ordinary suburban street, when the extraordinary truth burst into the inadequate confines of my soul and I *knew* I was forgiven. In a moment my life was forever changed as I was overwhelmed with the *truth* of God's forgiving love.

This is the work of the Holy Spirit. He reveals the reality of the truth. The ultimate intention of the Holy Spirit is to guide us into the truth of the glory of God. He wants to baptise us into the reality of God himself. Through the Holy Spirit we are not just those who read about and mentally assent that God is good. Rather, as the Psalmist writes, we are those who, "*Taste* and *see* the Lord is good" (Psalm 34: 8).

The Holy Spirit glorifies the Son

As the Apostle Peter has it elsewhere, "he has given us his very great and precious promises, so that through them you may participate in the divine nature" (2 Peter 1: 4). What could this possibly mean? The comment concerning this passage offered in one study Bible reads, "participation in the divine nature does not indicate that Christians become divine in any sense but *only* that we are indwelt by God through his Holy Spirit."[xi] The word 'only' here is a bit of an understatement. *Only* indwelt by God through his Holy Spirit is all: what a terrible disappointment! Did I miss something here, or does it really mean *indwelt by God?* The answer to this question is a resounding 'Yes!'

As Jesus explained concerning the Holy Spirit, "He will glorify me because it is from me that he will receive what he will make known to you. All that belongs to the Father is mine. That is why I said the Spirit will receive from me what he will make known to you" (John 16: 14-15). Which begs the question, "What is it that belongs to Christ that the Spirit will make known to us?" The answer — once again — is the relationship that Jesus has with the Father. Through the Holy Spirit, not only do we cognitively understand the truth of the relationship between Father and Son; *we participate in it.*

The Spirit ushers us right into the very circle of love, friendship and life that runs through and between the Father and the Son. The Holy Spirit glorifies Christ by revealing the interior reality of his relationship with the Father, and the Holy Spirit is most eminently competent to do so because he is the Spirit of their relationship. The Holy Spirit not only fills and connects the Father and Son, he *is* the connection between them.

The Spirit of Love

Have you ever been in the home of a couple who have an especially wonderful marriage, and encountered the extraordinary atmosphere created by their relationship? It's as if it were an almost tangible presence; as if the space between the husband and the wife creates a safe haven for real relationships and love to be fostered. A perfect place for a family, really.

I believe these kinds of unseen and immeasurable connections are more real and substantial than the bodies or the houses we live in. Physicists over the last century or so have come to recognise the universe itself is mostly made up of the mysterious immeasurable stuff that exists in the space between things, rather than of the things themselves. Of course, this shouldn't surprise us when we remember that the God who created it all is Father, Son, and Holy Spirit, living in an eternal life of relationship and that creation is the overflow of their love.

The real God is not a dispassionate, detached deity in the likeness of Zeus or 'The Force.' Those gods are nothing more than human constructs projected onto the darkness of our ignorance. The real God is Father, Son and Holy Spirit. The real God is an eternal dynamic community of love and the Holy Spirit is the infinite intermediary who fills and overflows the connection between the Father and the Son. This connection is so profound that the Father and the Son mutually *indwell* one another by the Spirit. In Jesus' own words "the Father is in me, and I in the Father" (John 10: 38).

A Wonderful Mystery

All this is an inconceivable mystery. I believe one of the reasons so little has been written about the Holy Spirit is that words *literarily* fail us. It's like trying to shovel hot lava with a wax spade: it's just not possible to really capture the glory of relationship with words. This may explain all the similes and metaphoric language the biblical writers used when speaking of the Holy Spirit: he is variously spoken of as being like a river, water, fire, wind or a dove. Other times, the Spirit is described as being breathed, poured out, hovering, brooding over, filling, baptising, falling upon, and more. All these create an image of movement, vitality, warmth and life.

The Holy Spirit glorifies the Father and Son by admitting us into the dynamic of their living relationship. By the Holy Spirit, we discover that we're positioned right in the middle of the love and vitality that passes endlessly between the Father and the Son. I believe this is just what Jesus was meaning when he said to his disciples, "how much more will your Father in heaven give the Holy Spirit to those who ask him?" (Luke 11: 13). Jesus was saying the Father is eager to share the love around. He wants you in the family!

The Power of Pentecost

This is exactly the kind of thing Jesus told his disciples to expect on the Day of Pentecost: "On that day you will realize that I am in my Father, and you are in me, and I am in you" (John 14: 20). This is another one of those verses we can read and then so easily skip over, but I encourage you to have another long hard look at what Jesus is really saying here. By the Holy Spirit, the disciples (and you and me) are enabled to see and dynamically encounter the life and love that Jesus has always known with the Father. In the same way that Jesus is in the Father, he is also in us, sharing his union with the Father with us. By the Spirit we are connected to the very same circuit of love that Jesus knows and lives in.

Pentecost was the beginning of a new era in human history, and the one hundred and twenty men and women in the upper room that day were the first to fully realize the implications and the reality of participating in the divine nature. No longer was the divine nature something they merely observed from the outside. By the Holy Spirit, the words Christ had prayed a few short weeks previously were now becoming a living reality (John 17: 20-26).

They were utterly, wonderfully, magnificently loved! They were drunk with it, filled and overflowing with the beauty and glory of it all! Little wonder they spilled onto the streets declaring to everyone and anyone that love had come to town. History was altered; reality was different; and as far as the disciples of Christ were concerned the whole world had tilted on its axis!

When Peter attempted an explanation he seized upon the words of the prophet Joel saying that this was what Joel had predicted; this was the day of the Spirit when God had said:

> I will pour out my Spirit on all people.
> Your sons and daughters will prophesy,
> Your young men will see visions,
> Your old men will dream dreams,
> Even on my servants,
> Both men and women,
> I will pour out my Spirit in those days,
> And they will prophesy.
>
> — Acts 2: 17-18

The Spirit had indeed been poured out and they were unable to stop their mouths overflowing with the immense reality of the love of God that coursed through their bodies. They realized, just as Jesus had said, that "I am in my Father, and you are in me, and I am in you." They were not merely caught up in a religious mania of evangelical zeal; nor had they simply put their collective finger into a divine power socket that transformed them into robotic preaching machines.

Instead, the drabness of stunted humanity was swept aside as they were arrested with a new vision for life. These were people compelled by palpable love. Not just any love; but exactly the same love that Jesus knows with the Father. That's what it really means to be filled with and baptised in the Holy Spirit.

D.L. Moody, the famous evangelist of the Great Awakening, described his experience of being baptised in the Holy Spirit with these words,

> ...I kept crying all the time that God would fill me with his Spirit. Well, one day in the city of New York — oh what a day, I cannot describe it, I seldom refer to it. It is almost too sacred an experience to name... I can only say, God revealed himself to me, and I had such an experience of his love that I had to ask him to stay his hand.[xii]

Notice how Moody describes his encounter with the Holy Spirit primarily as an overwhelming experience of the love of God.

All this is the work of the Holy Spirit, and none of it can be obtained by intellectual acrobatics or disciplined piety. Only the Spirit can make reality of these things. All we can do is simply let God love us as we trust the truth the Holy Spirit conveys to us and drink it in.

Neither is there a one-size-fits-all manner in which we encounter the Spirit. Just as each person experiences love or joy in ordinary life consistent with their emotional makeup and personality, so it is when we encounter the Holy Spirit. What really counts is the realization of love, not a particular outward behaviour or phenomenon.

Glorified Humanity

On one occasion Jesus foretold of the outpouring of the Spirit saying, "Let anyone who is thirsty come to me and drink. Whoever believes in me, as scripture has said, rivers of living water will flow from within him" (John 7: 37-38). John explained it this way, "By this he meant the Spirit, whom those who believed in him were later to receive. Up to that time the Spirit had not been given, since Jesus had not yet been glorified" (John 7: 39). But why was the giving of the Holy Spirit delayed until Christ was glorified?

The simple answer is this: the Father was waiting for the incarnation to be fully played out and reach its conclusion. Only Jesus has lived a complete and full human life, knowing the Father all the way from birth to death, and beyond: all the way to his ultimate glorification to the right hand of the Father *as a human being*. The Holy Spirit could only confer the fullness of this lifetime of true and glorious humanity upon us after Jesus had fulfilled the Father's plan through his life, death, resurrection and ascension.

Spirit of Adoption

The apostle Paul was able to write about all this with a certain amount of perspective post Pentecost. In the famous eighth chapter of the Roman epistle he writes,

> For you did not receive a spirit that makes you a slave again to fear, but you received the Spirit of sonship and by Him we cry out "Abba, Father!" The Spirit himself testifies with our spirit that we are God's children.
>
> — Romans 8: 15-16

There's a lot to see in this single verse. Paul is underscoring the amazing truth that we really are children of God sharing in the sonship of Jesus Christ himself and the Holy Spirit confirms what Jesus has made true.

The phrase, "Spirit of sonship" is particularly significant. The word 'sonship' can also be translated as 'adoption.' For most people of a Western mindset, adoption is seen in fairly neutral terms. However, in the Roman Empire, the ceremony of adoption was a significant event that would usually be carried out in a public forum. It was a way of letting the world know that *this* child is a legitimate daughter or son, and rightful heir of the father's estate. *This* child must be honored and treated with all the respect due any biological son or daughter.

We really are Children of God

Many times I have met believers who cannot accept the idea that they are really children of God. Forgiven and tolerated servants maybe — *but children of God?* No way! Nevertheless, the Holy Spirit, according to Paul, whispers to our souls that we really are legitimate children of God (Romans 8: 16). Notice there is an implied double witness here. The Holy Spirit "testifies with our spirit that we are God's children." It is as if the Spirit is confirming what our own soul was created to know. As Young's translation of this same passage has it, "The Spirit Himself endorses our inward conviction that we really are the children of God."

I recall seeing a video some time ago of a middle-aged man which recorded his reaction to the manufactured terror of an exceptionally frightening roller-coaster ride. Within a few moments the poor man was reduced to tears as he begged hopelessly for the ride to end — but it only got worse. Eventually he cradled his own head in his hands as he muttered the words, "Oh God, oh God, oh God..." in a repetitive mantra. Apparently it's not all that unusual for a person subjected to extraordinary stress, such as the heat of battle, the throes of sickness, or relationship breakdown, to involuntarily cry out, "oh God" or "mummy" or "daddy" in a similar fashion.[xiii] I can't help wondering if this phenomenon is in some way connected to "our inward conviction that we really are the children of God." Sometimes stress unmasks the real person inside and we discover who, or *whose*, we really are.

Whatever the case, the Spirit of sonship empowers us to connect directly with the love of God, and we find ourselves spontaneously calling God, "Father." Again, this is not merely a theological acquiescence so much as deep-seated recognition of an essential truth. This exclamation is the cry of Jesus Christ himself flowing from his relationship and his knowledge of the Father. No one in history ever dared to refer to God as *their* Father — let alone "Abba." To do so implies very real intimacy and confidence of identity. Yet, by the Spirit, we are able to voice the very same cry as the Son of God because by the Spirit we have a share in *his* sonship.

Paul goes on to conclude this passage saying, "Think what that means. If we are his children we share his treasures, and all that Christ claims as his will belong to all of us as well" (Romans 8: 17).[xiv] There are many things that Christ can claim as his, but top of the heap has to be his knowledge of — and oneness with — the Father. And by the Spirit we are given "the mind of Christ" (1 Corinthians 2: 16) to see and know what the Son sees and knows of the Father.

Glory Now – More Glory Later

You could be reading this and saying to yourself, "Sounds good, but if all this is so true and wonderful why is life so hard and painful?" Good question. We shall consider this in more detail in a later chapter but for now let me put it as succinctly as possible.

The Spirit does not change our circumstances or alter our past, but he does connect us to the love of God and gives us hope for the future. As Paul has it, "When you believed, you were marked in him with a seal, the promised Holy Spirit, who is a deposit guaranteeing our inheritance until the redemption of those who are God's possession."(Ephesians 1: 13-14). It's like being engaged to be married: you're already connected to the one you love, and enjoying the relationship, but the best is yet to come. No matter how hard things get, by the Holy Spirit the ultimate destiny is never in question.

As Jesus explained to his disciples shortly before his crucifixion, he would never abandon them or leave them as orphans in the world because, by the Holy Spirit, he would be with them forever (John 14: 16 -18). He wrapped up his final discourse to the disciples with these words "I have told you these things, so that in me you may have peace. In this world you will have trouble. But take heart! I have overcome the world" (John 16: 33). And by the Holy Spirit we can do precisely that — take heart.

PART TWO

Glory and Humanity

6

GLORY IN CREATION

A painful past

When I lived in Sydney I often had the opportunity to show international guests around the attractions of the city. One of the favourite destinations for many visitors was the landing site of the first Europeans on the eastern seaboard of Australia, arguably one of the most important historic sites in the nation. The intrepid explorer Captain James Cook (then Lieutenant Cook), famously took his first steps on Australian soil at this site and changed the course of history. The location of this event is now set aside as a National Park where visitors can tour the historical landmarks. On one occasion I took a British visitor with me who could be described as a history buff. I had been to the landing site many times before but this time I began to view it through the eyes of an overseas visitor.

What I saw shocked me.

On the way out to the landing we passed by a sewage farm, then through an industrial area, and then through a rundown suburb under the main flight path of one of the world's busiest airports. Finally we arrived at the park. First impressions were disappointing. The whole area had an air of neglected indifference about it. Overflowing rubbish bins, weeds and graffiti all conspired to dampen any anticipation we might have had for what was in store.

Even this did little to prepare us for what we were about to witness. The supposed site upon which Captain Cook first set his foot on Australian soil is actually a tiny island of rock embedded in the beach just a metre or two from dry land, and upon this rock a memorial plaque has been erected to commemorate the event. When my British friend laid eyes on this site, he was astonished to see an angler fishing from the rock. More scandalous still, this indecorous fisherman was using the plaque as a cutting board to dismember a hapless squid with his rusty knife.

Being a local I thought nothing of it, except to make a mental note for future reference that squid might be the secret bait to use at this venue. But my British friend was aghast! He wondered, "Why isn't this man being arrested and dragged off to prison for the rest of his natural life?" It was all incomprehensible to him. In any other country a site of similar significance would be protected by around-the-clock security guards, surrounded with magnificent gardens and well maintained tourist facilities. So, what on earth was going on here?

I believe the answer lies with Captain Cook's first-time encounter with the Aborigines who challenged his landing. Spears were thrown and guns fired in a short but tragic encounter between European explorers and east coast Aborigines. This was to set the tone for an unhappy history that saw the demise of the aboriginal peoples of Australia through disease, genocide, and neglect. Naturally enough, Australians are not particularly proud of this aspect of their history and even now the shame of our forebears' sins hangs heavily on the national psyche.

Created for Glory

Similarly the site where humans first set their foot on earth has also become a point of shame, a reminder of 'paradise' lost. It's not a proud moment in human history.

Yet the story starts promisingly enough, as we have already seen, with God fashioning humanity as the glorious masterpiece of his creation. So glorious, in fact, that humanity was actually created in the image of God, in his likeness (Genesis 1: 26). This doesn't mean that we physically resemble God, but more accurately that the glory of God is somehow inherent to our nature. The essential nature of God as love is therefore reflected in us, giving us the capacity to love and be loved.

This makes perfect sense when we read the very next verse: "So God created mankind in his own image, in the image of God he created them; male and female he created them" (Genesis 1: 27). For a human being to be in the image of God he or she must be a 'they.' *They* must be in relationship to really be capable of reflecting the image of God. We are what we are in our relationships; a human being who has no true relationships can only experience a stunted form of humanity. This is the first clue to the trinitarian nature of God's glory in creation.

What's more, this beautiful bond of love between the Father, Son and Holy Spirit is at work sustaining every aspect of creation. It's not split between 'sacred' and 'secular' bits. Creation is one whole, connected thing, made for interaction, relationship and love. Augustine, a well-known early church theologian, explained that we ought to therefore expect to see 'vestiges' of the Trinity in *all* creation. These vestiges are not just the residual 'fingerprints' of God. He didn't merely finish the creation and then kick it off into space as an independent entity or something to be viewed from a distance. As the apostle Paul sees it,

> For in him all things were created: things in heaven and on earth, visible and invisible, whether thrones or powers or rulers or authorities; all things have been created through him and for him. He is before all things, and in him all things hold together.
>
> — Colossians 1: 16-17

Creation is in Christ and Christ is in creation. He is involved and present to creation; always has been, and always will be. This is most especially true of humanity, "For in him we live and move and have our being" (Acts 17: 28). Adam and Eve were created to be far more than merely representative reflections of the nature of God in creation, or carriers of the 'divine spark.' It was always intended that they would bear the image of God in creation by being intimately included in the circle of love and fellowship with the Father, Son and Spirit.

Even now, despite the dark clouds of the fall, the brightness of this truth still manages to break through to remind us of the glory we were originally made for, and the depth of connection we are meant to live in. Sometimes we catch glimpses of it in the attachment of a family, or the oneness of a husband and wife, or in the face of friendship, or the cohesion of a community. Something inside us knows that these are the very things that give purpose and meaning to life.

I was once asked to write a list of the ten most exciting things I have ever experienced, and alongside it a list of the ten most meaningful things I have ever experienced. Remarkably, not one thing on my two lists matched. The most significant things are not necessarily the most exciting. For example, I recall a time when one of my sons wandered up to me, sat in my lap and nonchalantly said, "I love you Dad." That may not be the most exciting thing in the world, but in my mind at least, it was a truly meaningful moment. It's the connection we experience in our relationships that gives colour and depth to our lives because creation is fundamentally relational.

Glorious Vocation

Not only did God make Adam and Eve to be beautifully connected in fellowship with him, he also gave them a glorious vocation to "Be fruitful and increase in number; fill the earth and subdue it. Rule over the fish of the sea… and over every living creature" (Genesis 1: 28). We were made to have an ongoing participation in God's creativity. Human beings are not only spectators of the creation but partners in it with God. It was intended that we work with God, filling the earth with his image and "taking care" (Genesis 2: 15) of creation as priests and rulers (Revelation 1: 6).

When God finished the creation, everything was beautiful and functioned magnificently and cooperatively. The brightest jewel in this glorious world was Adam and Eve. So innocent and beautiful were they that "Adam and his wife were both naked, and they felt no shame" (Genesis 2: 25). How could they feel shame when they had nothing to hide and everything about them shone with the beauty of God? They weren't only physically naked but emotionally, socially and spiritually naked as well. Imagine it: Eve could ask Adam what he was thinking and he would tell her in detail and even explain what he was feeling! Then Adam would listen to Eve with an empathetic ear for hours at a time and even ask for more information! They had no secrets and withheld nothing from one another. They lived in perfect communion with God and one another, and the rest of creation as well. What a world!

Then something went horribly wrong.

Tainted Glory

Nothing discernible had changed on the outside but something substantial had changed on the inside. For the first time Adam and Eve experienced shame and "they realized they were naked; so they sewed fig leaves together and made coverings for themselves" (Genesis 3: 7). Adam and Eve had forfeited their glory. Now their nakedness, instead of revealing their glory, exposed the lack of it. Worst of all

Adam and Eve were so ashamed they hid from God when they heard him "walking in the garden" (Genesis 3: 8).

So what went wrong? Put simply, Adam and Eve took the very thing that made them what they were — their undiluted relationship with God — and traded it for a lie. When the Serpent tempted Adam and Eve he said "you will be like God" (Genesis 3: 5). Not just in the image of God but *as* God, autonomous and self-sustained. The Serpent deceived the primal couple into the belief that they could live independently of God (Genesis 3: 3-5); so Adam and Eve became twisted and corrupted. Like a glove without a hand, a sparkplug without an engine, a lock without a key, Adam and Eve became purposeless and futile. As one theologian put it,

> Man as creature, son and subject correlates with God as Creator, Father and King. Whilst he depends upon God, his humanity is authentic. If he tries to become more than what it is to be a Man then the burden of trying to be more than human is intolerable. In so-called 'god-ness' a Man loses his 'man-ness.'[xv]

Since our glory is to be at one with God in his love, sin is therefore not just a matter of breaking rules, so much as attempting to live without reference to the sustaining love of God — to go it alone. The outcome of 'living' independent of God is death on every level: physical, spiritual, social and ecological.

Paradise Lost

Adam and Eve's first taste of death was their expulsion from the garden. In their fallen state they were no longer fit to live in Eden; it would have been a torment for them. The way back to the garden is guarded by powerful cherubim,[xvi] and a flaming sword (Genesis 3: 24). Throughout history many people have tried to sneak back past the cherubim in a vain endeavour to set up some kind of utopian re-creation of the original garden. I'm thinking of communism, humanism, capitalism, and, dare I say it, every kind of 'God-ism' as well. But, all these 'isms' have been unerringly decapitated on the edge of the sword.

And still the 'garden' is where we all yearn to be, and now the entire human race experiences a kind of spiritual homesickness: an unquenchable thirst for glory. Maybe this is why we are moved when we witness glorious moments that stir the coals of our primeval memories, such as when a bride walks down the aisle on her wedding day, at the birth of a baby or when we witness an impossible victory. All these are reminders of 'paradise lost' and the glory we were originally created to live in.

I well remember poignant moments such as standing on a beach or a mountain top, watching the sunset after a magnificent day spent with friends sharing good times, when, for the briefest of moments, it was as if the celestial curtain lifted on a heavenly wind, and allowing me to momentarily gaze into the very meaning of creation. In these moments I often experienced a deep sadness; a sweet nostalgic sense of loss. I was incapable of explaining these emotions at the time, but have since come to recognise them as a longing for 'home.'

False Glory

However, if we can't find our true home we usually end up trying to make some sort of facsimile of it out of the flotsam and jetsam of the fall. Have you ever opened the fridge and peered in hoping you will discover some soul-satisfying morsel, 'the bread of life' — so to speak? But no matter how many times you look it's the same old wilted lettuce and stale leftovers. We eat it anyway because there's no other choice.

The prophet Jeremiah had something similar to say about the nation of Israel.

Has a nation ever changed its gods?
(Yet they are not gods at all.)
But my people have exchanged their glorious God
  for worthless idols.
Be appalled at this, you heavens,
  and shudder with great horror, declares the LORD.
My people have committed two sins:
They have forsaken me,
  the spring of living water,
and have dug their own cisterns,
  broken cisterns that cannot hold water.
— Jeremiah 2: 11-13

Jeremiah here explains how Israel had fallen into the same error as Adam and Eve by attempting to live independently of the true God. In doing so, they cast aside their vital connection to God himself: the 'spring of living water.' In a similar way we will settle for glory substitutes in life and 'dig our own cisterns, broken cisterns that cannot hold water.' The Bible calls this idolatry; we sometimes refer to it as addiction. Whatever you call it, it doesn't really satisfy.

The apostle Paul summed it up perfectly when he wrote of the devastating effects on human beings when they attempt to go it alone:

> For although they knew God, they neither glorified him as God nor gave thanks to him, but their thinking became futile and their foolish hearts were darkened. Although they claimed to be wise, they became fools, and exchanged the glory of the immortal God for images made to look like mortal human beings and birds and animals and reptiles.
>
> — Romans 1: 21-23

...And shopping centres, and share markets, and prestige cars, and a perfect marriage, and academic degrees, and the admiration of our peers, and, and, and, and — anything you can imagine. None of these may be wrong in themselves, but anything — even a thought — can *become* an idol, and idols are deeply enticing and deceptive. They promise freedom but deliver slavery; they promise life but deliver death. We stumble from one idol to the next hoping to finally find the elixir for the soul, but it never works. The thirst just gets stronger and the darkness grows deeper.

Eventually, the painful reality of the loss of glory drives us to invent all kinds of 'fig leaves' to cosmetically *cover up* what we are or *make up* for what we aren't.[xvii] Notice how Adam immediately tries to justify himself and even blames God for his predicament saying, "The woman *you* put here" made me do it (Genesis 3: 12). Every culture in the world has come up with some kind of 'fig-leaf' religion or self-justifying philosophy to cover-up their loss of glory.

Trouble in Paradise

The outcome of this breakdown in relationship with God was a consequent breakdown in relationship between Adam and Eve which culminated in a curse: "Your desire will be for your husband," God said to Eve, "and he will rule over you" (Genesis 3: 16). The meaning of the word 'desire' has been much talked about and debated over the years and no one really knows exactly what it means; but it has been suggested that it could be something like "you will look to him as the one who will supply your needs." If this is true then it explains the terrible dilemma that Eve found herself in. Her independence from God put her in a compromising dependence upon Adam. This, in turn, put Adam in a position of falsified power that gave him the capacity to lord it over Eve.

Sadly, the appalling record of women being used and abused by men throughout history bears ugly testimony to this curse. This 'curse' is not something that God imposed upon Eve, but was the consequence and outcome of her decision to ignore her essential need for dependence upon God.

All this would be bad enough, but it gets worse. Enmity sprang up between humanity and the rest of creation as well.

Unauthentic Humanity

Originally Adam and Eve were delegated as 'lords' over creation when their authority flowed from their appropriate relationship to the author of creation. We can get an inkling of what that may have been like when we take a look at the perfect man, Jesus.

Have you ever read the story of Jesus crossing Lake Galilee with his disciples, when a powerful storm hit them? The disciples were panicking — in fear for their lives — while Jesus slept untroubled on the deck. Eventually they could take it no more and woke Jesus from his slumber saying, "don't you care if we drown?" Unperturbed, Jesus turned and commanded the wind and the waves, "Quiet! Be still!" and immediately, all became completely calm. (Mark 4: 35-41). Was Jesus doing a 'God- stunt' by reaching beyond the limits of the incarnation when he rebuked the waves? No! He simply commanded the elements on the basis of his authentic humanity: the same kind of humanity that Adam and Eve originally had in Eden. The fall robbed Adam and Eve of their authority.

Imagine an army captain in command of a regiment of soldiers, who after some time begins to take his authority for granted. Eventually he decides to shake off the restrictions of military life and resigns his post. Soon after he meets a man and commands him to run an errand for him. But the man tells him to "get lost" in no uncertain terms. The 'captain' is deeply offended, but being large and strong he is able to use force and coercion to get his way. Without the authority of the army he is just a common thug bullying his way by brute strength.

Similarly, Adam and Eve soon realized that the creation would no longer collaborate and cooperate with them. Initially the creation was bountiful and generous with plants "pleasing to the eye and good for food" (Genesis 2: 9), but after the fall it begrudgingly gave up its produce "through painful toil" and began to sprout "thorns and thistles" (Genesis 3: 17-18). Now we have the legacy of extinctions, polluted rivers, droughts, vermin of various kinds and all the other blights and plights that plague the planet, to say nothing of the creatures 'red in tooth and claw'[xviii] competing with and eating each other.

Nowhere Else to Turn

However, human beings, even in their most distorted depravity essentially remain bearers of the image of God (Genesis 9: 6). We are still what we are, no matter how much we are marred by our rebellion. Even a mirror smashed into a thousand pieces continues to reflect the image of the one looking upon it, and even now, God continues to look upon the 'thousand broken pieces' of our fallen humanity. Indeed we desperately *need* to be 'looked upon,' or as Lewis has it, "noticed by God,"[xix] because our humanity is only authentic as we know him and are known by him. Thus our thirst for glory cannot be satisfied by anything other than God himself. The Amplified version of the Bible beautifully captures the significance of this idea in the book of Ecclesiastes,

> He has made everything beautiful in its time; he has planted eternity in men's heart and mind, a divinely implanted sense of purpose working through the ages which nothing under the sun, but only God can satisfy.
>
> — Ecclesiastes 3: 11

The frustration and pain of disconnection only deepens our need for glory and eventually turns us God-ward.

It's only then that we discover God has never turned his back on us. Like a child who refuses his or her parents' love, any feelings of separation are self-induced. In the garden God called out to Adam and Eve with the question, "Where are you?" to which Adam answers, "I was afraid because I was naked; so I hid" (Genesis 3: 9-10). The problem wasn't with God, but with Adam. It was his own shame and diminished humanity that made him afraid and incapable of relating to God.

The Promise of Glory Restored

Embedded in this story is a short verse, often overlooked, but full of meaning and hope: "The LORD God made garments of skin for Adam and his wife and clothed them" (Genesis 3: 21). Here we find the first hint of good news: God was immediately at work to redeem his lost children from their shame. God's provision of these temporary garments foreshadow the eternal garment he would later clothe humanity in — Jesus Christ.

We need much more than forgiveness of 'sinful deeds' to restore us. The only true remedy for human shame is re-glorification: a boundless forgiveness, a deep cleansing and a complete restoration of all our proper relationships with God, one another and creation. As we shall see, God has been relentlessly coming for us through all of history with one goal in mind: to restore us to glory.

7

GLORY IN COVENANT

'You just love them,' Logic

Some time ago I watched a fascinating documentary about the life and times of one of Australia's senior police commissioners. At one point, the journalist asked the commissioner's wife about a painful episode in her and her husband's life when their teenage daughter was arrested and convicted of dealing drugs. "What did you do when your daughter was convicted of this crime?" he asked.

The commissioner's wife looked up with tears in her eyes and replied, "What can you do? She's your daughter, so you just love her don't you?"

There's no way of logically explaining this kind of love. It's impossible to fully comprehend. Yet it seems to me we are all finely tuned to the pitch of this kind of love.

The Bond of Love

I certainly remember tuning in to the pitch of this love at the births of my own children. I felt a profound but inexplicable connection with each of them the moment they were born. The birth of my second child, Tess, is particularly illustrative.

I know fathers are not meant to say such things about their daughters, but when Tess was born she was not a particularly attractive baby. She was kind of bluish, had a large strawberry birth mark on her forehead and her left ear was bent sideways because she had been constantly holding it in the womb. More importantly, I knew what I was getting myself into as I already had a one-and-a-half year old son at home. I knew Tess was about to cost me piles of money, sleepless nights and soiled nappies. Yet I instantly — and profoundly — loved her. To me, she couldn't be more beautiful. From the moment of birth (if not before) I was aware of a powerful but invisible bond between Tess and myself. The same was true with all my children — even though there is no apparent logic to this connection or any kind of immediate reciprocal benefit to me.

I have talked with many people who were adopted as infants, and even though they were happily raised in their adoptive family, they felt an undeniable nagging desire to reconnect with their flesh-and-blood family. Later in life, many of them have done exactly that, as they set out to re-discover their original family. These invisible but powerful bonds are all around us.

The Bond of Covenant is the Glory of God

The biblical word 'covenant' actually means 'bond.' In the Bible, covenants were usually instigated with a formal recognition of a special connection between two parties, and confirmed with the giving of vows and taking of oaths — a bit like a wedding service today. Covenants could be between God and people, two individuals, two families, two tribes or two nations, but covenant bonds do not necessarily need to be written and organised to exist.

My children have a kind of unspoken covenant with their mother and me. They are the literal offspring of the bond or covenant that exists between us. All this is a dim reflection of the unspoken covenant that has eternally existed in the Trinity. The Father, Son and Holy Spirit are the true original 'family' and creation is the offspring of their bond, so creation itself is fundamentally covenantal. Covenant is, therefore, a magnificent manifestation of the glory of God.

Rightly understood, covenant is the backdrop of the entire Bible: a multi-millennia-long-saga of God 'just loving us.' The scriptures are divided into the testament of the Old Covenant and the testament of the New Covenant. Both the old and the new point in the same direction, and in them we discover God's goal for history is an extraordinarily domestic and familial one. God, apparently, is not so interested in being 'superstar-king of the cosmos' as being the Father of a family. Don't get me wrong: he *is* king — but he's the Father-King, the humble Lord, the master who serves and loves his family. God the true Father is ultimately out to gather his children to his table, to bring them back home.

The often repeated covenant motif, "I will be your God and you will be my people," and its derivative, "I will dwell with you and you will dwell with me" is, I believe, the primary theme of the Bible and indeed of history. Unless we grasp this covenantal foundation of the biblical story we are almost certain to miss the point of *everything*.

Covenant and Contract

All true covenants are based on a 'you just love them' kind of logic rather than the mutually agreed exchange of goods and services that you might expect in a contract. Sadly however, covenant is often confused with contract. This is hardly surprising given so many relationships have a contractual basis: "You do this for me and I'll do that for you; you be my friend and I'll be yours."

Many people see spiritual life in this light, and have projected the idea of 'contractual obligation' onto Christian faith. Conditional 'ifs' and other prescripts for spiritual life such as, "if you have enough faith, you'll be healed" or "when you truly repent, God will forgive you" engender a misleading contractual understanding of our relationship to God.

True covenant is based in love not obligation. God is not obligated, conditioned, or compelled to love us. He is completely free in his love and graciously chooses to love us whether or not we respond. It's "I *will* be your God" not "I am required to be your God." And we in turn are not forced to respond, but graciously free to respond in kind.

Marriage is meant to reflect this kind of understanding and is the closest thing to a formal covenant still in existence in the Western world. In a traditional wedding service the prospective husband and wife make covenant promises to one another such as, "I take thee to be my wedded husband or wife, to have and to hold from this day forward, for better or worse, for richer or poorer, in sickness and in health, to love and cherish, till death us do part."[xx] Notice how these promises are unconditional and apply even when things are worse, or poorer, or sick. Such is the nature of a covenant. Ideally, at least.

Said and Unsaid Covenant

In the Bible, the first formal mention of covenant takes place just after the flood. God declared to Noah and his family, "I now establish my covenant with you and with your descendants after you and with every living creature that was with you — the birds, the livestock and all the wild animals, all those that came out of the ark with you — every living creature on the earth" (Genesis 9: 9-10). The word 'establish' here is important because it doesn't mean that God is initiating something new. 'Establish' means reiterate, or underscore, or ratify. In other words, God is saying to Noah, "That which has always been I am now formally underscoring and re-establishing with every living creature." All the formal covenants in the Bible are actually enlargements of the unspoken covenant of creation. [xxi]

Notice the covenant is not only with human beings, but with "all life on the earth" (Genesis. 9: 17). This, I believe, is the mysterious thing we almost grasp when confronted with glory in creation. I remember a scene from the Academy Award winning film, 'American Beauty' when Ricky, in a moment of pensive reflection, gives a moving soliloquy while watching a simple video he had made of a plastic bag caught in an eddy of wind:

> It was one of those days when it was a minute away from snowing and there was this electricity in the air. You could almost hear it….and this bag was just dancing with me…and like a little kid it was begging me to play with it for fifteen minutes. That's when I realized that there was an entire life behind things and this incredibly benevolent force that wanted me to know that there was no reason to be afraid — ever…The video is a poor excuse I know, but it helps me to remember — I need to remember…sometimes there's so much beauty in the world I feel like I can't take it anymore and my heart is just going to cave in.

C.S. Lewis calls this the "inconsolable secret,"[xxii] that mysterious but not quite concealed truth of the glory of God permeating every piece of creation. The covenant is being worked out on a grand scale: from the galaxies and stars right down to the sub-atomic particles. He is sustaining and nurturing every fragment of his creation for the sake of the covenant. Absolutely everything is contributing toward the grand goal of the covenant that, "I will be your God and you will be my people."

Universal Truth

This all-encompassing influence of covenant struck me some years ago as I watched a documentary about the personal life of Saddam Hussein. At one point, the program depicted the former dictator embracing and playing with one of his nephews. His face was one of sheer delight and his nephew responded in kind. Even a despot needs the connection of covenant relationships. "Family values" are not the preserve of conservative middle-class Christians. They're bedrock to all humanity.

Some psychologists have argued that the traditional family unit ought to be dispensed with because it has been the cause of so much pain and dysfunction. [xxiii] Surely, however, it could be reasoned that it is precisely *because* we are made to live in the context of covenant relationships that when they dysfunction we get seriously messed up.

I have personally heard the heartbreaking stories of hundreds of people who have been variously mangled in the machinery of dysfunctional families. Indeed all of us have been subject to imperfect families, and yet we cannot really function without them.

Social workers whose task is to oversee the welfare of children from disintegrated families have explained to me that — aside from abusive circumstances — most children are better off in a somewhat dysfunctional family than a faultless institution. Each child has a fundamental need to be raised in a covenant community, whether this be a foster family or a biological family.

God wants a Family

The story of God making a covenant with Abraham is one of the key stories concerning covenant in the entire Bible. In it we get an even more profound vision of God's covenantal glory and the goal of history. There's an amazingly common familial thread running through the unspoken covenant of creation and the formal covenants put in place with Noah and Abraham. All three of these covenants feature an obvious mandate to produce families (Genesis 1: 28, 9: 7, 15: 5), but where does this mandate lead?

The covenant promises that God declares to Abram (later renamed Abraham) certainly gives us some potent clues (Genesis 15: 1-5). The first promise is as astonishing as it is wonderful. "Do not be afraid, Abram. I am your shield, your very great reward" (Genesis 15: 1). God promises *himself* to Abram! This is the initiation of the first clause of the covenant motif, "I will be *your* God."

God then goes on to promise that Abram would father a child and have innumerable descendants. This is the fulfilment of the second clause, "you will be *my* people." A little later in the story God explicitly reaffirms these promises saying, "I will establish my covenant as an everlasting covenant between me and you and your descendants after you for the generations to come, to be your God and the God of your descendants after you" (Genesis 17: 7).

A Really Big Family

These promises are not only for the physical descendants of Abraham, the Jews. Rather, Abraham was to be the fountain head of a river that would eventually swallow the entire sea of humanity. This brings to mind the enigmatic prophetic saying, "For the earth will be filled with the knowledge of the glory of the LORD as the waters cover the sea" (Habakkuk 2: 14). The prophet Habakkuk was saying that God's glory would be revealed through his faithfulness to his covenant people beginning with Abraham, then his descendants, then to *all* the peoples of the earth. All this was embedded in the call of Abraham when God declared, "I will bless those who bless you, and whoever curses you I will curse; and *all peoples on earth will be blessed through you*" (Genesis 12: 3). God chose Abraham to touch *every* nation, tribe and family on earth. The fulfilment of this promise is ultimately brought to completion in Jesus Christ.

I remember catching an insight into these truths at a beach in the city of Sydney. Sydney has one of the most multicultural populations on earth and also has an uncommonly strong connection with the beach. On any hot summer's day, the beaches are invariably crowded. Whole extended families stake out their position on the sand and spend the entire day camped out on the beach.

As I looked down from the car park at the press of human flesh massed on the sand below me, I could see a cross-section of the world's cultures. Every imaginable skin colour from lily white (rapidly turning bright pink) to spectacular black was represented in this snapshot of humanity. Right then, I had an unusually poignant experience. I found myself deeply distressed at the plight of all these people I imagined were disconnected from God and at the impotence of the church to make a noticeable impact. Could the Gospel really make the smallest difference to the larger part of this gathered mass of humanity? What has Jesus Christ to do with all these people?

Just as my feelings of disillusionment were about to peak, they were replaced by a new sensation — an insight from heaven that had me peering into a mystery beyond words. I suddenly saw that every single person on that beach *was* somehow connected with Jesus Christ. The power of his life, death and resurrection are somehow being poured out on the entire population of the world. No one is excluded from the love, promise and influence of Jesus Christ. It was a most eerie and unusual experience. I'm not saying everyone is therefore aware of Jesus, or embracing these things, just that Jesus Christ is much bigger than our best imagination can invent (1 Corinthians 8: 5-6).

The God of People

Another important covenant motif used twenty eight times in the scriptures is God's own self-designation, "I am the God of Abraham, Isaac and Jacob" (Exodus 3: 6, for instance). This short phrase tells us a whole lot of things about God and also about us. It tells us God is not aloof and detached, he's the God of real flesh-and-blood people. I remember when my two youngest sons were at school I would often be referred to as "Jack and Max's dad." To the children at the school, I was more than 'just some guy.' I was known in terms of my covenant relationships. Likewise, God is not just some god, he's the God of Abraham, Isaac and Jacob, and by inference all those descended from them. God is known in terms of his bond with real people and glorified through his covenant faithfulness.

All of Grace

The other thing this motif reveals is the utterly grace-full nature of the covenant. "Abraham, Isaac and Jacob" are the first three generations of the 'people of God.' They set the pattern for everybody who is counted as a 'child of Abraham.' Take Abraham for instance, he was nobody special. He was just another idol-worshipping-pagan minding his own business when God called him. Abraham did nothing to elicit God's attention — it was God's free choice.

If we move on to Isaac, we discover he was born miraculously because of an extraordinary intervention by God. His parents, Abraham and Sarah, were as "good as dead" (Romans 4: 19) when he was conceived. As if to underscore the point, Jacob was also the result of impossible pregnancy. Can you see what this means? The *entire* line of Abraham is therefore the result of gracious call, a miraculous intervention, and an impossible possibility!

I have Jewish blood in my ancestry which means that I wouldn't physically exist if God hadn't done what he did with Abraham, Isaac and Jacob. Israel is the upshot of the utterly graceful act of God. This of course is true of everyone who is counted as a child of Abraham, whether a physical descendant of Abraham or a gentile included by grace through faith (Galatians 3: 8-9).

Certainly that's how Paul saw it as he tried to persuade his Roman readers, "it is not the children by physical descent who are God's children, but it is the children of the *promise* who are regarded as Abraham's offspring" (Romans 9: 8). Paul goes on to conclude, "It does not, therefore, depend on human desire or effort, but on God's mercy" (Romans 9: 16). John the Baptist even went so far as to say that God can make children of Abraham out of rocks if necessary (Luke 3: 8). I'm fairly sure there are more than a few of these in churches I have visited, to be honest.

What does all this have to do with the glory of God? Everything! God is revealed as a God like no other. He is the God who is faithful to the covenant and steadfast in love. We cannot make ourselves members of the family of God;

it's a free gift. We are "children born not of natural descent, nor of human decision or a husband's will, but born of God" (John 1: 13). All we can do is trust God.

Free but not Cheap

Most children are completely unaware of the tremendous sacrifice their parents have made to give them their place and space in the family and in life. I remember when I was a new father having a fresh insight and appreciation for my own parents halfway through changing a particularly horrible nappy — my parents did *this* for me! Our membership in a family may be given to us free, but it's never cheap. This is particularly true of our inclusion in the family of God.

In the Bible, covenants were normally sealed with the sacrifice of animals. In our civilized, sanitised world it can be difficult for us to appreciate the importance of blood sacrifice in the ancient world. Blood signified both the seriousness and cost of establishing a covenant. Even so, the Old Testament covenant between God and his people was only a temporary arrangement put in place until the instalment of the New Covenant. The blood of animals only paid the interest on the loan but not the principal, so to speak (Hebrews 10: 3-4), but the blood spilled to make the New Covenant possible was the life of the Son of God. It's what we remind ourselves of every time we take Communion. In Jesus' own words, "This cup is the new covenant in my blood, which is poured out for you" (Luke 22: 20). It may have been poured out freely, but it cost everything.

The blood spilled to establish the new covenant is the ultimate expression of the glory of God. As the writer of the letter to the Hebrew has it,

> But we see Jesus, who was made lower than the angels for a little while, now crowned with glory and honor because he suffered death, so that by the grace of God he might taste death for everyone. In bringing many sons and daughters to glory, it was fitting that God, for whom and through whom everything exists, should make the pioneer of their salvation perfect through what he suffered.
>
> — Hebrews 2: 9-10

The main purpose of the spilling of Christ's blood was to bring many sons and daughters to glory, to restore the human race to their place in the family of God. This brings us to the cross of Christ where all the covenant promises find their fulfillment and where the glory of God fully shines.

8

GLORY IN THE CROSS AND THE RESURRECTION

Glory Stronger than Death

"He is risen!" declares the preacher on Easter Sunday morning and all those in earshot joyfully reply, "He is risen indeed."

It's a happy, hope-filled Easter tradition, and the declaration never seems to grow tired. But, even as a child, I desperately wanted more information. *How* and *why* did Jesus rise from the dead? To which the reply was usually, "God raised him from the dead." True though this may be, the answer always left me cold for some reason.

The reason became clear some years later when I was a student in a public speaking course. There, I remember being taught some of the essentials of a good story. The main character of the tale must overcome a series of obstacles through a process of spiritual growth, dogged persistence, sheer bravery, incredible ingenuity, or whatever it takes to climb the mountain, win the war, best the opposition, land the job or gain the heart of the beloved. The story is ruined if the 'cavalry' simply march in and save the protagonist from the conflict. That's precisely how I felt whenever someone rolled out the pat answer about the resurrection. There had to be more to it than some arbitrary decision on the part of the Father. Jesus rose from the dead. Brilliant! But *how* did he prevail and *why* was it so?

I believe the answer to these questions is once again entirely contingent upon the integrity and virtue of the bond of love between the Father and the Son — the glory of God. This immediately exposes another controversy which also seriously troubled me as a child.

The centrepiece of many Easter sermons, rather than being all about the bond of love between the Father and the Son, was commonly quite the opposite. Apparently, according to many preachers I listened to as a boy, in the moment of Jesus' death, the bond of love between the Father and the Son was severed. I knew intuitively this simply could *not* be. Surely if the relations of the Trinity flounder — even for a moment — the universe would collapse upon itself?

Just recently, in a Bible-study, discussion turned to this same subject, when somebody called into question the things being said about the unbroken bond between the Father and the Son and quoted from a book they had been reading that very morning, "He paid the horrible debt that sin had accrued in the universe. God the Father, who is unable to look on sin, *had* to turn his back on him. Jesus therefore plunged into the darkness of sin and endured the awful suffering of atonement *entirely on his own...*" or words to that effect.

Sadly, I have heard this line of reasoning all too often.

This notion is rooted in an extreme version of the atonement theory called 'penal substitution' which essentially has the Son being punished by the Father as a means of satisfying the 'Father's righteous judgement against sin' according to the prescriptions of the Law. The main problem with this idea is that it seems to be saying that Jesus is not really God. At the very least it's saying Jesus is somehow subordinate in nature to the Father. To me this is a flat denial of the Trinity which blithely hacks away at the very foundation of the Creeds and the Faith.

How is it possible that the Father is too 'holy' to look on sin, while the Son is able to bathe in it? Is the Father somehow more 'holy' than Jesus? If Jesus is paying off the debt of sin to satisfy the Father's demand for moral righteousness according to the Law, then *who* is paying off Jesus? Isn't Jesus equal with the Father? Isn't the first thing we say about God all about the oneness of the Father, Son and Holy Spirit? In any case, if Jesus is paying the penalty of sin to satisfy the Father it makes the Father out to be essentially unforgiving and sets up an irreconcilable contradiction within the Trinity.

When Jesus went to the cross he wasn't fixing up something in God the Father. Atonement was never aimed at God: it was aimed at the human race — at you and me. The cross has nothing to do with placating God and everything to do with transforming us.

Orbiting the Glory of God

Before the seventeenth century, everybody 'knew' the sun orbited the earth. That is, until Galileo probed the night-sky with his telescope and discovered that it was actually the other way around. The universe could no longer be thought of with earth-centred cosmology. Likewise if our understanding of the crucifixion and resurrection is to stand it must orbit around the glory of God, not the problem of human sin.

Athanasius, the great fourth-century theologian and one of the principal architects of the Nicene Creed, had exactly the same kind of dispute with Arius, a popular but misguided leader in the early church. Arius believed God the Father was superior to the Son and that the Son had not always existed but was 'created' by the Father at some point. Arius' reasoning was based on what he observed with earthly parents and their children, but Athanasius argued that the moment we begin thinking about God starting with our own human point of view we are bound to end up creating a mythology instead of a theology;[xxiv] we end up projecting onto God our own fallen human ideas.

Similarly, if our 'theology' of atonement begins with the problem of human sin instead of the glory of God we are bound to repeat Arius' mistake of projecting fallen human logic onto God. That's the problem with the notion of Jesus paying off the Father. It ignores the glory of God and creates divisions of inequality within the Trinity.

I'm not saying that Jesus has not borne the consequences of our sin. He has. But the *way* he has borne it is far more profound than a legal transaction. I could ramble on forever about these things, but let's take a closer look at what really happened on the cross and in the resurrection.

Paradox

Maybe you have heard of the 'Seven words of the Cross?' These are a compilation from the gospels of the seven things Jesus said while on the cross. Of the seven, there are two essential passages which at first glance appear to be somewhat contradictory.

The first is recorded in the gospel of Matthew: "About three in the afternoon Jesus cried out in a loud voice, *"Eli, Eli, lema sabachthani ?"* (which means, "My God, my God, why have you forsaken me?")" (Matthew 27: 46). The second is penned by Luke: "Jesus called out with a loud voice, "Father, into your hands I commit my spirit." When he had said this, he breathed his last" (Luke 23: 46).

There's a paradox here. On the one hand Jesus appears to have been abandoned by the Father, while on the other he trusts the Father in the moment of death. The apparent gap between these two words has created room for all kinds of mythologies. Was Jesus *really* forsaken by the Father? Isn't it possible that Jesus was simultaneously experiencing the distress of human despair and loss, as he staggered under the weight of our corruption and sin, while he also trusted his Father to the end?

We must keep in mind that the sentence, "My God, my God, why have you forsaken me?" is actually a quote from Psalm 22:1, which itself is the first verse of a typically paradoxical Psalm. In the first half of the Psalm David expresses deep emotional pain and despair, yet the second half is full of hope and joy. The conclusion of the Psalm is all about the faithfulness of God in the midst of difficult circumstances. In David's words, "For he has *not* despised or scorned the suffering of the afflicted one; he has *not* hidden his face from him but has listened to his cry for help" (Psalm 22: 24). If this is true for David, how much more is it true for Jesus Christ?

This paradox should not amaze us. Most believers I have talked with have had their most profound experiences of God's grace while in the grip of suffering and emotional tumult. Suffering and the faithfulness of God are certainly not mutually exclusive. The life of Christ was constantly suspended between these two paradoxical poles. In the incarnation, Jesus experienced everything we go through, *both good and bad*, and in the crucifixion, Jesus simultaneously spanned the entire width between the two furthest extremes of human existence, from intimate closeness to the Father all the way to infinite alienation. Yet, through it all, the bond of love between the Father and the Son was kept elastic and alive by the Holy Spirit, even as it was being stretched beyond what would be the breaking point in any other human being. The integrity of the bond between Father, Son, and Holy Spirit remained unbroken through every possibility of human life.

More than a transaction

Our view of these things will be very much influenced by our view of the nature of God as Trinity, and by our understanding of what the incarnation is really all about. As we have already seen, the primary purpose of the incarnation was bigger than forgiveness of sin. Jesus came to enable the human race to know the Father just as he knows the Father.

If we take the limited view that the primary purpose of Christ's incarnation was to become a suitable sin-bearer and substitute penalty-taker then we reduce the crucifixion to a merely external transaction between the Father and Jesus on behalf of humanity.[xxv] However, the blood of Christ is far more than sin detergent: it represents his entire life.

Two Scars

There are two different scars on the body of Jesus: a navel scar and nail scars, and both are equally vital for our salvation. When Jesus took on human flesh, it wasn't only with a view to the final six hours on the cross. In reality, the crucifixion was the grand finale of a perfect human life — the only perfect life ever lived. When an athlete triumphantly breaks the tape at the end of a marathon, it's not only the final stride that counts. That moment of triumph is dependent on *every* single step from start to finish. In the same way, every second of Jesus' life — from two cells in the womb of Mary all the way to final breath on the cross — is a vital link of an unbroken chain of faithfulness to the Father that is vital to the resurrection.

The cross is that final step, the last link, the ultimate and deepest descent into the fallen human condition. There's no particle in all the possibility of humanity that Jesus has not penetrated and then permeated with his faithfulness to the Father. By the Holy Spirit, Jesus has taken his connection to the Father into the furthest reaches of sin and death; no matter how deep the soul of any human being has descended into darkness, Jesus has gone deeper still.

The fourth century bishop, Gregory Nazianzus famously said "That which was not assumed is not healed; but that which is united to God is saved."[xxvi] By this, he meant that it was necessary for Jesus to not only bear the consequences of sin, but also to assimilate every aspect of our humanity in order to reconfigure and restore what was lost. *Jesus not only died the death we should have died: he also lived the life we couldn't live,* and it's the life he lived that gave him power over death.

The Integrity of the Life that Jesus Lived

I once knew a professional fisherman in Darwin who fished well offshore with specially designed and very expensive nets for Spanish and Spotted Mackerel. Unfortunately, the tangled fish attracted the unwanted attention of large Tiger Sharks which not only ate the fish but also shredded the nets.

But the fisherman had a solution.

Once the nets were set he also cast several large metal drums into the water sporting a length of chain and a baited hook. Invariably the sharks would soon find the baits and hook themselves against the buoyancy of the drum. The sharks were big enough and strong enough to easily pull the drum under water but the buoyancy of the drum would eventually draw the shark back to the surface. The shark would dive, and dive, and dive again: but in the end it was futile. So long as the drum remained intact the shark was doomed. After a few hours the sharks were dead: problem solved. Unless, of course, you happen to be a Tiger Shark.

This story may help to illustrate how the integrity of the bond of love between the Father and the Son is the key to the defeat of death. Imagine the shark is death (that shouldn't be too difficult to do). The drum represents our life and the baited hook is sin. Death is attracted to sin and drags the drum under water. The problem we have is that our 'drums' are all rusted and full of the holes of our fallen humanity. When death drags us down we stay down.

Jesus on the other hand has no sin and so death is unable to touch him (John 10: 18; 14: 30). Nevertheless he deliberately baits his hook with our sin. Death now has access to Jesus and he too is dragged under by death, but Jesus has the buoyancy we lack. His 'drum' is watertight and firm. Death tests him but the virtue of his sonship and the glory of his faithfulness to the Father are simply stronger than death. Death is doomed. The resurrection is inevitable. As the apostle Paul has it, "Death has been swallowed up in victory" (1 Corinthians 15: 54).

Gloriously Human

Let us not forget that Jesus is fully human in all this. Jesus is God become man: the man who is God, and as such he has fully identified with our humanity with all the limitations and weakness of fallen human flesh. The difference between him and us is his unbroken fellowship with the Father. For the entire span of his human life this bond between the Father and the Son must remain intact if the resurrection is to be effected.

Remember when Jesus was tempted by Satan in the wilderness (Luke 4: 1-12)? The temptations directed at Christ were not moral temptations so much as inducements toward relational denial — to go it alone. Satan tried to get Jesus to act independently of the Father. It was the very same temptation he successfully employed to undo Adam and Eve. If Satan had succeeded the incarnation would have been invalidated and the resurrection impossible. Notice at the end of the temptations, the scripture records, "When the devil had finished all this tempting, he left him [Jesus] until an opportune time" (Luke 4: 13). The most opportune time, of course, was the final six hours on the cross. But even in that moment when the bond of love between Father and Son was stretched to its fullest under the weight and horror of broken humanity, Jesus nevertheless trusts the Father all the way to the end.

As the apostle Peter wrote, "When they hurled their insults at him, he did not retaliate; when he suffered, he made no threats. Instead he *entrusted* himself to him who judges justly" (1 Peter 2: 23). His final word on the cross was therefore, "Father, into your hands I commit my spirit" (Luke 23: 46). Jesus stared down the horror of death and overcame the temptation to doubt the Father's love.

Death to Death

The bond of love between the Father, Son and the Holy Spirit is the exact opposite to the bond-breaking power of death. Life is all about connection, while death is about disconnection. At a purely physical level death breaks the bond between body and spirit, husband and wife, parent and child and an individual and their community. Physical mortality is only one form of death and we all experience its bond-breaking devastation long before the demise of our mortal bodies.

'Death' can end marriages, families, friendships, partnerships and fellowships even while we're alive. Ultimately death, in all its forms, makes a mockery of all our human ambitions and crushes our hopes to dust. No one in history has successfully stood against it. That is, until the jaws of death attempted to bite through the unbreakable bond of eternal life, and all its teeth were shattered.

Charles Wesley captured the sense of this in his famous hymn '*And can it be*' when he wrote,

'Tis mystery all! The immortal dies;
 Who can explore this strange design?
 In vain the first-born seraph [Satan] tries
 To sound the depths of love divine.
 'Tis mercy all! Let earth adore,
 Let angel minds inquire no more.

The first-born seraph's bid to trip Jesus up was disastrous: he could not find an outer edge to the limitless love of God. He was doomed to fail.

A Glorious New Day

The resurrection is, therefore, the inevitable outcome of this glorious triumph; the medal ceremony after the victory, so to speak. The gates of Hades have finally fallen to the unbroken bond of love between the Father, Son and Holy Spirit. The resurrection is, therefore, a new beginning for humanity and the whole of creation. For the first time ever, the grave has been denied as Jesus has triumphed over death as a *human being*. A representative of Adam's race has *finally* made it through and now we all share the spoils of the battle won.

In the words of T.F. Torrance

> He stood in our place, taking our cause upon him, also as Believer, as the Obedient one who was himself justified before God as his beloved Son in whom he was well pleased. He offered to God a perfect confidence and trust, a perfect faith and response which we are unable to offer, and appropriated all God's blessings which we are unable to appropriate. Through union with him we share in his faith, in his obedience, in his trust and appropriation of the Father's blessing: we share in his justification before God. Therefore when we say we are justified by faith, this does not mean that it is our faith that justifies us, but we in faith flee from our own acts even of repentance, confession, trust and response, and take refuge in the obedience and faithfulness of Christ.[xxvii]

Hope for Us All

Now our place in the family of God is secured and assured. The New Covenant has been permanently guaranteed by the blood of Christ (Hebrews 10: 12-18). He has done what none of us could do. All we can do is "take refuge in the obedience and faithfulness of Christ." This is a pretty good definition of faith. Real faith starts with God, not with us.

If you were brought up in the church you would almost certainly have been taught about faith through the story of David and Goliath (1 Samuel 17). Doubtless, you will remember how David, a mere lad, took on the champion of the Philistine army, Goliath — a nine-foot-tall warrior. Goliath had been taunting the Israelite army for days, trying to provoke one of them to fight him. None of the Israelites was either brave or stupid enough to do so.

When David came to visit his brothers on the battlefield he begged for a chance to fight Goliath and eventually the king consented to his reckless request. Long story short, David took Goliath down with his slingshot and then the whole Israelite army joined the battle and the Philistine army was routed.

I can still hear my Sunday-school teacher saying "…and if we have faith like David we can defeat the 'Goliaths' in our lives too." Faith was taught as taking risks and being brave in the name of the Kingdom of God, and when we do, good things happen. That may be all well and good, but to be honest, I don't really identify with David even though he's my namesake. The people I identify with are the foot soldiers in the Israelite army scared out of their wits by Goliath.

To me 'Goliath' is the combined power of sin and death. Even on my best day there is no way I am going to take him on. But then David — a type of Christ if you like — steps onto the field and wins the impossible battle. This is exactly what Jesus has done to death. Now, like the ancient Israelite army, we have a share in *his* victory over death.

We can no more take credit for that than we could take credit for enjoying the sunshine on a beautiful day. Our enjoyment of the day doesn't make the day beautiful; it's the other way around. The beauty of the day allows us to enjoy it. As Kruger has it: "Faith has no power without truth. Without reality, without Jesus, faith is simply a form of magic where we try to weave our spell over someone or wrest the cosmos to our will apart from Jesus."[xxviii] Our faith does not make a thing true — rather, the truth enables us to believe.

Genuine faith can only exist in the light of the faithfulness of Christ. Only this kind of faith can stir up genuine hope: the hope of glory.

9

GLORY AND SUFFERING

A Reason to Live

Some days are not as good as other days.

Australia Day, January 26, 2005 is a day I will never forget. At around nine o'clock in the evening my friend Dan and I were travelling as passengers in a taxi-van on a highway in Goa, India, where we had been speaking at a local Bible college. I remember the soft colours of the fading light, the hum of the wheels on the road and chatting with Dan. The very next thing I remember is waking from what I thought was a horrible nightmare about being in a car crash, but notions of nightmares were instantly crushed as a granite-block of pain slammed me with the realisation that the nightmare was real. Dan was dead. My body was broken. It was a bad day.

Anyone who has travelled on the roads of India or indeed any Asian country will doubtless have many tales of numerous near-death-experiences involving buses overtaking around blind corners, or trucks travelling at break-neck speed on crowded streets. Sadly, these stories are all too true and our taxi had ploughed head-on into a truck travelling on the wrong side of the road. The impact was enough to mash the front half of the taxi and fuse the two vehicles together before tipping off the road and sliding down a steep embankment into the bush below. Dan was killed instantly along with the driver of the taxi and I was well on my way to joining them with a shattered right femur, broken left hip joint, crushed vertebrae, fractured ribs and several deep lacerations to the lower legs. Blood loss and shock would soon claim my life without medical help.

For the next three hours I wavered on the edge of consciousness; teetered on the edge of life. They were the longest hours of my life. It wasn't the first time I had been confronted with the possibility of my own death, but having so long to think about it affected me profoundly. The pain was unbearable and death was a tempting escape. I somehow knew I could have deliberately made the choice to slip off into the relief of unconsciousness, and then simply slide off the edge of life.

The notion of 'life flashing before your eyes' in the throes death has become something of a cliché but an experience just like it actually did happen to me. The faces of friends and people I knew seemed to be paraded before me. Then the faces of my wife Catherine and our four children began to come more clearly into focus. For the first time I began to think how my death would affect them. My youngest was only ten at the time and I intuitively knew he would be devastated if I died. "I *have* to live" I thought to myself. Something inside me changed and I resolved to do whatever it took to cling to life. Now I had a reason to look past the pain; something to live for.

I was eventually cut from the wreckage and rushed to the local hospital for life-saving surgery. Then began the long road to recovery, which is a story in itself. Looking back all these years later, I now realize it wasn't just the surgery that saved me. It was hope that gave me the will to endure. You've probably heard it said, 'where there is life, there is hope' but the opposite, 'where there is hope, there is life' is even truer I believe. The stronger the hope: the greater the capacity to endure.

Hope of Glory

In the scriptures there is a very clear connection between hope and perseverance. For instance in the fifth chapter of Romans, Paul writes,

> And we boast in the hope of the glory of God. Not only so, but we also glory in our sufferings, because we know that suffering produces perseverance; perseverance, character; and character hope. And hope does not put us to shame, because God's love has been poured out into our hearts through the Holy Spirit, who he has given us.
>
> — Romans 5: 2-5

Paul goes right to the greatest hope of all, "the hope of the glory of God." This hope is the only hope that can endure *anything* and will never disappoint us.

The meaning of the biblical word for 'hope' is not equal with wishful thinking or whistling in the dark. Rather it's a real and confident expectation of good to come your way. The hope of glory is a real and confident expectation that one day we will look on the face of God and be fully indwelled by the love shared between the Father and the Son, in fellowship with the Holy Spirit. What we have tasted by the Spirit now will be fully realized in the life to come. This hope is not based on the mettle of our spirituality, nor is it dependant on the circumstances of our lives. Our confidence is secured by the presence of Christ himself. As Paul has it elsewhere, "Christ in you, the hope of glory" (Colossians 1: 27).

Testing Hope

Not all hopes are equal. We all have hopes for various things in our lives that are legitimate and important. We have hopes for family, friendships, health, well-being, career, security and love. In addition we have hopes for our country, community and the whole world. But all these hopes have a breaking point. Just like fishing line, they will break when put under too much strain.

When fishing line is manufactured, it is made to a particular 'test' strength. Some line is ten kilogram test for instance, some is five, and so on. When the line is strained beyond that weight, it will break — an unfortunate experience I have endured many times when fishing. The same is true of our life and hopes. For example, no matter how strongly we hope for enduring good health, it's inescapable that the day will eventually come when sickness will break our hope.

In this way, suffering tests our hopes and determines their various 'test' strengths for us. We discover, through the crucible of pain, the worth and weight of our hopes. Suffering inevitably reveals the penultimate nature of our normal hopes. None of these hopes are stronger than death, but how would it be if we had a hope that was never destroyed, no matter how much strain it was put under? It would be like fishing with line that could not be broken.

Imagine you are fishing from the rocks when you hook a large and powerful fish. The fish dives under a rock and you can feel the line scraping over the barnacles and weed — but it doesn't break. Then, the fish takes a scorching run and the line stretches and stretches — yet it still doesn't break. Time and again, the fish strains the line, but no matter what happens the line simply cannot be broken. After a while, you may start to relax and trust the line will not fail. The more times the line is put to the test, the more confident you become.

I believe this is exactly what Paul means when he refers to perseverance producing character. The word 'character' here has the sense of 'proven substance' about it. Suffering reveals the substance of our hopes. The hope of glory is the only hope that remains intact, even in the face of death; it's the ultimate hope. The end effect being — even greater hope. Can you see what Paul is saying? Suffering, rather than destroying the 'hope of glory,' actually underscores it.

Suffering forces us to reconsider truth and meaning in every sphere of our lives. It crushes all our self-referential constructs of reality, false securities and utopian fantasies, and helps us see what really matters. Suffering also teaches us that death is not the last word and reveals the hope of glory as greater even than death. In the end, even the suffering will end while the hope of glory goes on and on. As Paul has it later in the same letter to the Romans, "I consider that our present sufferings are not worth comparing with the glory that will be revealed in us" (Romans 8: 18).

Nothing can Separate Us

Something else happened while I was trapped in the crashed taxi: I had a profound encounter with God. I cannot fully express or explain it, but even as I lay there in terrible pain surrounded by death, I *knew* God was with me. I paradoxically encountered the love of God in the presence of death in dimensions and in intensity impossible to describe. It was almost shocking to experience such grace in the middle of such pain. I have never felt so utterly desperate, and yet so utterly loved all at once.

Ever since that day I can honestly say I firmly believe that I am always loved no matter what. This is not a testimony to the strength of my faith, so much as a testimony to the reality of the love I encountered. This doesn't mean I'm walking on sunshine singing hallelujah every day: far from it! All I'm saying is that there's an undeniable confidence that the love of God is not altered by death or sorrow. The pain of those events, both physical and emotional, disarmed any doubts I may once have had about the love of God and the reality of the hope of glory. For the first time, the noise of my penultimate hopes were silenced, and in their place: the hope of glory.

I soon discovered that the experience I had is not as unusual as I initially thought. During the first few months after the crash I was confined to a wheelchair. Whenever I went into a public place such as a shopping centre or busy street I was commonly approached by all sorts of people, who would ask, "What happened to you?" Often they would listen empathetically to my story and then they would tell me *their* stories of disasters survived and tragedy outlived.

I count it an enormous privilege to have been granted the opportunity to hear the heart-breaking accounts of so many people. My wheelchair gave me passage into a kind of 'fellowship of suffering.' This fellowship is made up of ordinary people but each of them has an extraordinary story to tell. These are people whose bodies have been permanently wrecked, or who will never marry, or who will never have children, or who have lost children, or who will never see their home land again, or whose loved ones are long dead. The list goes on and on and on. Yet these same people would look me square in the face and say, "If it wasn't for the love of God I don't think I would have made it."

Anyone can say "God is good" when life is good. But there's something far more convincing when those same words are spoken by a person in pain. I once heard of a man who was confined to a hospital bed — his death-bed as it turned out — his body riddled with cancer. A friend asked him with a mixture of anger and defiance, "Where's your God now?" The man in the bed struggled to lift his emaciated body up onto one elbow. He caught the eye of his friend and said with a steady voice, "He's right here" as he placed his forefinger on his chest, before slumping back. End of argument.

No matter what anyone says, suffering can't ultimately control you, so long as you have an authentic hope — the hope of glory. This is exactly how Paul sees it as he writes,

"For I am convinced that neither death nor life, neither angels nor demons, neither the present nor the future, nor any powers, neither height nor depth, nor anything else in all creation, will be able to separate us from the love of God that is in Christ Jesus our Lord" (Romans 8: 38-39). This hope does not disappoint us.

Fortified Hope

Paul then goes on to explain that the hope of glory is much more than an intellectual concept or theological idea. It's a living palpable truth made real as "God's love has been poured out into our hearts through the Holy Spirit, who he has given us" (Romans 5: 5). The Holy Spirit gives form and depth to our hopes by giving us a foretaste of the glory that will one day become a magnificent shining reality.

It's a bit like the excitement and anticipation of landing a big fish before it's in the boat. In my home state one of the favourite angling targets are large, handsome, pink-coloured fish called Snapper. Unfortunately, small sharks and stingrays are also regularly encountered on the same grounds as Snapper and prefer the same baits as well. When an angler hooks a fish they are keen to know if they have hooked a much-prized Snapper or a much less desired shark. Once the fish is close enough to the boat the angler looks for 'colour.' The angler knows he or she is connected to a Snapper by the tell-tale flash of silvery-pink beneath the boat. This is something like what the Holy Spirit does for us. He gives us the 'colour' of glory long before we land it. Our hope is therefore confirmed and fortified by the Spirit.

The 'colour' we see by the Spirit is the colour of love shared between the Father, Son and Holy Spirit. The Holy Spirit gives us a taste of the 'milk and honey' from the 'Promised Land' while we are still wandering in the wilderness here and now. This is the way he fortifies our hope of glory.

Pie in the Sky?

This doesn't mean we just give up on this life now and sit around waiting for 'pie in the sky when we die.' Far from it! The hope of glory enhances and underscores the meaning and depth to all our penultimate hopes here and now. Without the hope of glory everything is ultimately pointless and futile, but with it, everything is re-minted with new depth and meaning. At one level the hope of glory means *nothing* really matters because whatever happens our destiny is secured by Christ, and nothing can ever take that from us. But at a whole other level it means *everything* matters. Everything is somehow connected and contributing to the grand purpose of glory.

In the end, nothing is wasted or insignificant. Everything, even things that appear, and in fact are, dreadful and evil, eventually leads us to our glorious inheritance. I'm not saying that *everything* is good or that everything happens for a purpose. However, I do believe everything works together *for* good and ultimately contributes to a purpose because God's essential nature is good and loving, and he will work with any and every circumstance to make that love known to us (Romans 8: 28).

No more Sleeps

A few years ago, I had the privilege of marrying a young couple in our church. It was a very long engagement and their anticipation was almost excruciating. Every time I saw them they would say something like, "Only sixty four more sleeps to go" as the agonizing countdown ground on. At length, the wedding day finally came and their mutual joy was manifestly evident. At the reception a small card had been placed on all the seats with a personal note to each of the guests. I opened mine and the simple message inside said it all, "No more sleeps."

The day will eventually come when there are "no more sleeps" for us, too. Until then, the hope of glory will keep us and protect our hearts and minds from whatever life throws at us (Romans 8: 24).

10

GLORY AND THE WORLD TO COME

Glory beyond the Grave

When I first started out in pastoral ministry, people often asked me, "What really happens to us when we die? What is the life to come going to be like?" To these questions I gave the standard answers I had inherited from my evangelical upbringing. But I never felt entirely at ease with the responses I was so confidently giving. "I ought to look into this and find out what the life to come is really all about," I thought to myself.

So, for the next couple of months I set about doing an exhaustive study of every verse in the Bible that even obliquely referred to life-after-death, and read every book on the subject I could get my hands on.

What I discovered was disconcerting.

It turned out almost nothing I had believed about the life to come was either true or biblical. Most of the things I had once believed owed more to the influence of Western culture rooted in Greek mythology than any kind of authentic biblical insight. As disconcerting as this all seemed at the time, there was, nevertheless, a positive upside. The actual truth is far and away better than the myth! It's well beyond the scope of this book to delve into all that detail here; suffice to say, the life to come is all about glory. [xxix]

A Word of Warning

The problem with talking about the life to come is that it's indescribable.

In my bachelor days I used to live with a friend who was completely colour blind — he could only see greyscale. Sometimes he would ask me to describe a colour to him, "Can you tell me what the colour blue looks like?" He would ask.

"Well, it's kind of like the sky on a clear day." I would reply.

"You mean light grey?"

"No, not really. It's more like the ocean in summer."

"Dark grey?"

And so it would go.

I just couldn't give him a useful answer. Trying to talk about the life to come can be a bit like that I'm afraid.

It comes as no surprise, therefore, that the Bible *only* uses metaphor and symbols to talk about the life to come. There are no literal descriptions of life after death anywhere in the scriptures. Instead we have wonderful metaphoric images of wolves and lambs feeding peacefully together (Isaiah 65: 25), of trees that fruit with riotous abundance (Ezekiel 47: 12), of streets paved with gold (Revelation 21: 21), and many more besides.

I'm always a little bit suspicious of any detailed or realistic visions of things beyond the grave. I prefer to say the life to come will be as different from this life as a tree is from its seed. All we have in this life is the 'seed' of glory by which to imagine the 'tree' of glory that one day will emerge from it (1 Corinthians 15: 37). It's therefore beyond us to fully grasp future glory. Nevertheless, the seed of glory we experience in this life has exactly the same DNA as the tree of glory we will one day experience in the life to come. This life and the life to come are deeply connected just as a tree is to its seed.

I can't help wondering if that's why we have those unbidden moments when beauty seems to spill over the retaining walls of our natural senses, to connect us with an intensity of insight and wonder too exquisite to explain. Lewis wrote of these moments as "stabs of joy,"[xxx] as if something from another dimension and of "incalculable importance" had penetrated the ordinariness of hum-drum life.[xxxi] But, just like waking from a dream that's so vivid you're certain it could never be forgotten, the memory of it fades to nothing in an instant: an indulgent fullness for a moment: a devastating emptiness in the next. Even so, these tantalising but intangible moments remind us the best is yet to come, with the restoration of all our proper relationships — to God, one another and creation: true glory.

Heaven comes to earth

Therefore, just as you might expect, all the biblical metaphors of the life to come point us in exactly the same direction as the hope of glory. One of the most significant of these is captured in the book of the Revelation where the apostle John describes seeing,

> The Holy City, the New Jerusalem, coming down out of heaven from God, prepared as a bride beautifully dressed for her husband. And I heard a loud voice from the throne saying, "Look! God's dwelling place is now among the people, and he will dwell with them. They will be his people, and God himself will be with them and be their God. He will wipe every tear from their eyes. There will be no more death or mourning or crying or pain, for the old order of things has passed away." He who was seated on the throne said, "I am making everything new!"
>
> — Revelation 21: 2-5

There is so much contained in this short passage.

For starters, you'll notice we don't 'go to heaven;' rather heaven comes to earth in the form of the 'Holy City.' Obviously, the city is not a literal bunch of buildings with skyscrapers, polluted rivers and traffic jams. In the Bible the word 'city' is used to describe a guarded community, a safe place to live and connect with a wider society (Psalms 107: 2-7). The Holy City is meant to be understood more in terms of a state of being rather than a geographical location.

This is borne out in the next verse, "God's dwelling place is now among the people, and he will dwell with them" (Revelation 21: 3). This is the final fulfillment of all those covenant promises we looked at earlier about God dwelling with his people and us dwelling with him. The metaphoric meaning is simply this: heaven and earth are no longer divided. God's place is now our place as well. As Peterson has it in the Message, "Look! Look! God has moved into the neighbourhood, making his home with men and women! They're his people, he's their God."

And what a home it is!

It's not a House, it's a Home

In the heart-warming movie, 'The Castle,' the main character, Darryl Kerrigan, is embroiled in a legal battle to defend his house from being bulldozed to make way for the interests of big business. In his defence he says, "It's not a house, it's a home. It's got everything: people who love each other, care for each other, memories — great memories. It's a place for the family to turn to, to come back to." I'm quite certain Jesus had something like this in mind when he said to his disciples, "My Father's house has many rooms... I am going there to prepare a place for you" (John 14: 2). In Bible language 'house of David' or 'house of Jacob' means the 'family of David' or the 'family of Jacob.' Jesus was saying, therefore, "In my Father's *family* there's a place for you."

Unfortunately, this important truth has been somewhat obscured by the erroneous translation of this same verse in the old King James Version which reads, "In my Father's house are many mansions." Subsequently notions of 'mansions in the sky' and 'castles in the clouds' have somehow embedded themselves into our collective consciousness and are bandied about with an air of unquestioned authority, but that's not what Jesus was meaning at all. The glory of the coming age is mostly about restored relationships, not luxurious housing estates in the suburbs of the Holy City.

'I am making Everything New!'

Back to our passage from Revelation where John declares, "the old order of things has passed away" and in its place, "everything new!" (Revelation 21: 2-5). The 'old order,' of course, refers to the regime of this broken world and its broken relationships. The 'new,' to the restoration and re-glorification of all things. Can you imagine a world where there's no greed or wastage, no rivalry or envy, no outsiders or insiders? A world where everybody is enthusiastically motivated to enhance the life of their neighbour? Where everybody is bursting with life and vitality? Where sickness and death have faded to nothing? Deep down we long for a world where these things are a shining magnificent reality.

Even though the reality of the life to come exceeds the limits of our imagination, the longing for 'heaven' is, nevertheless, universal. It's what everybody really wants — not just people of a religious bent either, but *everybody*. Often I see this longing portrayed in beautiful artwork, poetry, or lyrics.

Take for instance these lyrics from the song, "This could be heaven" written by Roger Taylor for the rock band, Queen.

Yeah, this could be heaven for everyone
This world could be fed, this world can be fun
This should be love for everyone,
This world should be free, this world can be one

We should bring love to our daughters and sons
Love, love, love, this could be heaven for everyone

I believe Tayor has faithfully captured the essential hope of 'heaven' here in terms of love and relationships. It's not about the geography and architecture, it's all about love. Who cares about mansions and streets of gold if you don't have love?

I recently saw a television program called "Q&A" in which a panel of prominent public figures are quizzed by members of the public. One member of the audience put this question to the panel:[xxxii]

"Can the panel comment on what defines a good life and a good death? How can a successful life be truly measured?"

To this Malcolm Turnbull, a man who had enjoyed great success both in business and politics replied,

Well, I've been lucky to have loved and been loved by a wonderful woman, Lucy, and our two beautiful children, and I have to say that everything else over and above that, every triumph, every attempt to triumph, whatever, is irrelevant compared to that. At the end of the day, when you boil it down, it's about love and it's about your family.

Surely the life to come will be measured in similar terms? Everything else will seem irrelevant compared to finally finding our place in the family of God and knowing we are loved and free to love.

Heaven on Earth

All this relates not only to humanity but the rest of creation as well. As we saw in the covenant with Noah, God has plans to glorify the entire creation, not just the human race. The creation as it is now is already beautiful beyond words, and yet in its current form is only a shadow of the reality yet to be! Certainly that's how the apostle Paul sees it when he writes of the life to come as a place where "the creation itself will be liberated from it bondage to decay" (Romans 8: 21).

Much of the magnificent diversity of the present age is the product of a broken creation, where plants and animals compete with and eat one another, each straining to secure their piece of the energy and minerals necessary for life, survival of the fittest and all that. How much more beauty and diversity will emerge in a world where the plants and animals actually collaborate and cooperate with one another instead? A world where each species promotes and makes room for the other?

To top it all off, humanity and creation will be in perfect harmony. Just as creation was implicated in our fall, it will be even more wonderfully implicated in our glorification! As we have previously touched on in the writings of the apostle Paul, "the creation waits in eager expectation for the children of God to be revealed" (Romans 8: 19), because then creation will liberated "from its slavery to corruption into the freedom of the glory of the children of God" (Romans 8: 21 NASB). Creation will have a share in the glorification of the children of God.

It's the great reversal of the glory lost in the fall of Adam and Eve. For the creation it will be the end of pollution, extinction and wasteful exploitation, and for us it will mean no more disasters, disease or death! What would a world where humanity glorifies creation, and creation glorifies us look like I wonder? One thing is certain: it will be a world vibrant with life that will foster never-ending possibilities for glorification.

Dynamic Glory

I recall seeing a cartoon about heaven by Gary Larson which depicted a man with a harp and halo sitting on a cloud apparently bored out of his mind. The caption of the cartoon read, "I wish I had brought a magazine." The real 'heaven' will be nothing like this of course. If it's all about relationships then the life to come could never be static. The process of glorification will never end.

In his second letter to the Corinthians Paul writes, "And we all, who with unveiled faces contemplate the Lord's glory, are being transformed into his image with *ever increasing glory*, which comes from the Lord" (2 Corinthians 3: 18). The phrase "ever increasing glory" is literally "from glory to glory" in the original language. This means that the more we see the glory of God the more we are transformed by it as we "contemplate the Lord's glory." Glory therefore begets glory in a never ending upward spiral. The process of glorification that has begun in this life will carry on into the next — only more so.

Elsewhere, John writes, "Dear friends, now we are children of God, and what we will be has not yet been made known. But we know that when Christ appears, we shall be like him, for we shall see him as he is" (1 John 3: 2). Can you see what

John is saying? We're already children of God, but there's so much more yet to be revealed. For the more we see God *as he really is*, the more we become who we really are, because our glory is inherently linked to the glory of God.

We don't become less the closer we get to God — we become more! Just as the Father, Son and Holy Spirit are everlastingly defined by their mutual indwelling of one another, so too will we be defined as we fall endlessly into the love of God. The more we see the glory of God the more distinct and glorious we will become. But here's a question: will we ever get to an end of knowing God or exhaust the depths of his glory? Of course not! As long as there is something new to know about God then the life to come will just keep on getting better and deeper without end. Boredom isn't even a possibility.

Heaven

'Heaven,' therefore, can be defined as simply as this — it's seeing God and being seen by him, knowing God and being known by him, loving God and being loved by him. In the Bible to 'see the face' of someone is akin to knowing them or being in their immediate presence. Which is what the apostle John is meaning when he goes on to write, "The throne of God and of the Lamb will be in the city, and his servants will serve him. They will see his face, and his name will be on their foreheads" (Revelation 22: 3-4). It's a beautiful metaphoric way of saying we will know God and be known by him. The more we see the glory of God the more glorious we in turn become, which enables us to see him even more deeply, resulting in even more glory – and so it goes – forever and ever and ever.

Little wonder John writes, "And he carried me away... and showed me the Holy City, Jerusalem, coming down out of heaven from God. It shone with the glory of God, and its brilliance was like that of a very precious jewel" (Revelation 21: 10-11).

This is our glorious inheritance.

PART THREE

Glory in Human
Relationships

11

GLORY IN MARRIAGE

A Fraught Conversation

Unless you spent the last decade or so asleep, you would be well aware of the highly emotive minefield that has sprung up around the world-wide conversation on gender roles and marriage. As far as I can tell there seems to be two mutually exclusive positions drawn up on either side of this particular conversation. On the far right wing we have those who hold a strongly hierarchical position believing men lead and women follow, with clearly defined gender roles. While on the far left wing we have those who hold an egalitarian position believing in unequivocal equality between the sexes, with androgynous gender roles.

I'd like to suggest that both these views are broken human responses to an age old problem, and that both are inherently flawed. Perhaps there's an entirely different way of understanding men, women and marriage that doesn't have its roots in the infertile soil of our flawed and broken humanity. Perhaps masculinity and femininity in marriage can be more suitably defined with a full-blooded vision of men and women created in the image of God? I believe that if we really want to get some idea of what the model husband or wife looks like then we must first take a long hard look at Jesus Christ.

The Model Husband

I once heard of a young man who took great pride in the fact that his wife often referred to him as 'the model husband' until he looked up the word 'model' and discovered that it meant, "a miniature replica of the real thing." Unfortunately men, as a rule, tend to have an entirely flawed view of exactly what constitutes 'the model husband.' This seems to be especially so of men brought up in the Church.

I've lost count of the number of times over the past couple of decades of pastoral ministry that men have rung me up insisting I come over to "tell my wife that she is not being submissive to me." I always accept the invitation in the sure knowledge I won't be saying a word to the wife and anticipate a contentious conversation with the husband instead.

The main reason for this seems to stem from an almost universal misunderstanding of the biblical picture of 'headship' and 'submission' portrayed in Paul's famous words in the fifth chapter of Ephesians where he writes,

> Wives, submit to your own husbands as you do to the Lord.
> For the husband is the head of the wife as Christ is the head

of the church, his body, of which he is the Savior. Now as the church submits to Christ, so also wives should submit to their husbands in everything. Husbands, love your wives, just as Christ loved the church and gave himself up for her to make her holy, cleansing her by the washing with water through the word, and to present her to himself as a radiant church.

— Ephesians 5: 23-27

Unfortunately most men conveniently overlook all reference to Christ in this passage and instead project their own fallen ideas of headship and submission onto it. This is hardly surprising given the broken role models to which we have all been exposed, to say nothing of the vested interest of men in maintaining the status quo of a power imbalance massively skewed in their favour.

The true husband

As far as Paul is concerned, we must see the relationship of the husband and wife in the light of the relationship between Christ and the Church. The key phrase in this passage is this, "as Christ loved the church" (Ephesians 5: 25). Once we understand what that looks like, then – and only then – can we begin to discuss what the model husband looks like.

Naturally this begs the question: "How *does* Christ love the Church?" The simple answer being: "By giving himself up for her" (Ephesians 5: 26). And as Paul goes on to write, "to present her to himself as a *radiant* church, without stain or wrinkle." The word 'radiant' here is the same word that's usually translated as glorious elsewhere in the New Testament. In other words Christ is bringing the church to her fullness, dignifying her, enabling her to be everything she can be, and letting her shine. Then Paul makes application of all this to the marriage relationship saying, "in the *same* way, husbands ought to love their wives" (Ephesians 5: 28).

Giving away the advantage

So how, exactly, does Jesus achieve this goal of glorifying the church?

As discussed in chapter three in the story of Jesus washing his disciples' feet, Jesus used his power to serve his disciples, not to lord it over them, or force his will upon them (John 13: 1-17). After he had practically demonstrated his love to the disciples he taught them, saying, "Now that I, your Lord and Teacher, have washed your feet, you also should wash one another's feet. I have set you an example that you should do as I have done for you" (John 13: 14-15). Obviously, following Paul's logic, this same principal applies to husbands in the marriage relationship.

The secret Jesus was teaching his disciples here was how to give away your advantage. Jesus didn't keep the power of his privileged position to himself; instead he freely shared it with his disciples and ultimately his bride, the Church. Keep in mind that the way Jesus Christ loves the church is precisely how the Father has eternally loved the Son. The Father shares all power with the Son, he totally trusts the Son, and holds nothing back from the Son, and the Son does the same for us. Rather than using his power to dominate and manipulate his bride, he uses it to elevate and reinstate her.

Real headship

This kind of 'headship' is light-years away from the pattern of authoritarian headship we are all so familiar with in this world. In Jesus' own words, "You know that those who are regarded as rulers of the Gentiles lord it over them" (Mark 10: 42). But he goes on to say, "Not so with you. Instead, whoever wants to become great among you must be your servant, and whoever wants to be first must be slave of all. For even the Son of Man did not come to be served, but to serve, and to give his life as a ransom for many" (Mark 10: 43-45). This means that an authoritarian style of authority must be regarded as unauthentic, because it isn't as the author intended.

Jesus refused to impose his will on the church by sheer force or power — even though he could have if he wanted to. Instead, according to Chrysostom "He brought her to his feet by his great care, not with threats, or violence, or terror, or anything else like that, but through his untiring love." Just like Paul, he logically concludes, "So also you [husbands] should behave toward your wife." In the Kingdom of God, power is meant to be freely given by those who have it to those who don't — which is very different to the way the world works.

Headship then, as Paul understands it, means being first in line to serve. The husband is therefore the 'prime minister' in the marriage — literally meaning: the *first servant*.

True Masculinity

This kind of purposeful *service* is not the same as placating *servitude*. Being first in line to serve can only occur at the hands of a secure man. What Paul is not talking about here is the castrated version of masculinity so often portrayed by popular culture in the form of a spineless weakling attempting to placate the woman in his life by giving way to her every demand. On the contrary, it takes a truly secure person to be genuinely humble; and a truly strong person to be genuinely gentle. Jesus is the perfect example of this.

Real masculinity initiates acts of service rather than placating by acquiescence. It doesn't take any kind of special qualities in a husband to passively give way to the demands of his wife, and any idiot can be a bully, but it takes a real man to truly serve and win the heart of a woman.

The Male Advantage

But why does Paul see the husband as first in line to serve rather than the wife? Why does he have different expectations for men than he does for women? The short answer is this: men are different to women. This is an obvious fact, but the differences between men and women go far beyond the effects of testosterone and oestrogen. There's a power disparity between men and women as well. The fall — as explained before — has handed men an unequal portion of the power pie, and the only way this imbalance can be properly resolved is with the conscious cooperation, and deliberate participation of men.

Unfortunately most men are blithely unaware that they are born with a whole stack of advantages that women simply don't enjoy. Which explains why elsewhere the apostle Peter writes, "Husbands, in the same way be considerate as you live with your wives, and treat them with respect as the weaker partner" (1 Peter 3: 7). The word 'weaker' here doesn't mean lesser so much as disadvantaged. Certainly that's how Petersen sees it as he translates this same verse like this, "Be good husbands to your wives. Honor them, delight in them, as women they lack some of your advantages."

What Advantages do Men have?

The most obvious advantage men have is physical strength. The mere fact of a man's larger frame and stronger physique can be intimidating for a woman let alone that a man has the option to bodily force his will — if push comes to shove. Sadly, and all too often, push *does* come to shove. Little wonder, then, that men are responsible for well over ninety percent of domestic violence. Is this evidence that men are somehow fundamentally worse than women? I think not. I believe it simply reveals the inherent power imbalance and therefore the greater opportunity men have to abuse their position. I've certainly talked with men who have been the victims of physical abuse in the less common circumstances where the wife has a physical advantage over her husband. For the most part, however, men have the advantage of physical strength.

Another obvious advantage men have is greater access to financial freedom. Pregnancy and the pitter-patter of little feet can have profoundly adverse effects upon a woman's career prospects and financial security. This, in turn, makes women more vulnerable and dependent upon their partners.[xxxiii]

It therefore comes as no surprise to learn that across the globe, women do the majority of the work, but get paid significantly less than men for the same roles. Even in the most developed nations, women get paid significantly less than men.

As a direct consequence of all this, entire cultures and systems have developed self-perpetuating systems that favour men over women. Even if women contest the 'system,' the energy and time it takes to scale these fences only serves to disadvantage them all the more. The only way women can achieve real equality with men requires that men be 'man enough' to share their unfair advantage. It really is that simple and yet that fraught.

Power Unawareness

Most men are born into the world with the fullest belief that the entire cosmos rotates on an axis which passes right through the middle of their body. Many men go through life expecting things to come to them or be done for them. To a large degree it inexplicably and unreasonably does. Studies have shown, for instance, that teachers naturally give more of their time and attention to boys in the class room than they do to girls no matter what the subject and no matter the sex of the teacher.[xxxiv] It's almost impossible for men to fully appreciate how much easier it is to be a man than it is to be a woman in this fallen world. In many ways it really is a man's world.

The problem for people with power is they have almost no perception of their privileged position or empathy with those who lack it. This is true not only between men and women but in every other power imbalance you care to name — such as the rich and the poor, employer and employee, teacher and student, governments and the people, healthy and sick, educated and uneducated, and a whole world of other categories besides. It reminds me of the famous words apocryphally attributed to Marie Antoinette during the famines in France under Louis XVI, "If they have no bread, let them eat cake instead."

The mind-numbing absurdity of this situation is exacerbated by the frustration people without power experience in trying to communicate their discontent to those who have it. I've certainly heard many a desperate wife tell me through tears something like this, "My husband's a really nice man, he's great with the kids, and I know he cares for me, but he just doesn't get what it's like for me. He just doesn't listen." Regrettably I seem to remember one of those women being my own wife at one, or possibly, many points.

Eventually, a woman without power feels forced to either give up and lie down or stand up and fight. An insecure husband will generally respond by either attempting to dominate his wife, or by retreating from her into his cave. Either way, he goes on getting his way to the detriment of the relationship.

Sadly, I have to confess to being culpable of exactly this sort of behavior in my own marriage and have often wished I could go back in time to visit the twenty-something-year-old version of myself and teach him some of these hard-won truths. Like most men however, I was utterly unaware of the unfair power advantage I had.

A Gradual Process

In fairness to men though, the hardest thing in the world for a person with power is to give it away. Only a secure and mature person can willingly give their power to another.

Change — if it comes at all — is therefore usually something of a gradual response over time. What follows is fairly generic and certainly not always true of all men — but there's sure to be something that many men can identify with nonetheless.

In my observation, most husbands go through three distinct stages in married life. Many a man initially gets married thinking he's doing his bride an enormous favour by simply marrying her and letting her join him on his journey through life. Most women, on the other hand, enter marriage believing they are entering a mutually collaborative partnership. It comes as something of a shock to a newly married woman that her husband isn't thinking like she does. Most young brides have no idea that their groom is ignorant of what a woman really wants. Fortunately this stage usually doesn't last all that long, especially if children are introduced to the mix. As the needs of a wife become more apparent, so the demands she makes on her husband increase.

The husband then enters the second stage of marriage which I will call the 'happy wife: happy life' stage. Through the crucible of existential suffering — which is to say through the onslaughts of an angry, nagging, unhappy wife, or a cold, unresponsive, distant wife — the husband reluctantly learns the expedient advantages of keeping his wife happy. For a while, this may work, but there's a world of difference between being forced to give, and being willing to give, and there isn't a woman on earth who will remain satisfied with this arrangement.

The husband sooner or later finds himself becoming exasperated by his wife's dissatisfaction. "What more does she want? I give her everything she asks for and more, and yet she's never satisfied" he reasons. But ultimately a woman wants something more than patronising support. What she really wants is to be loved: to be truly cherished, deeply known, and genuinely heard. A woman wants to be taken seriously as an equal partner in the relationship. The only way this can possibly happen is if the husband grows up and learns to freely share his unfair portion of the power pie with his wife. It takes a real man to do something like that — until then he remains a boy.

But here's the secret: far from diminishing himself in this process he actually becomes greater. I seem to remember Jesus saying something along these lines, "Whoever tries to keep their life will lose it, and whoever loses their life will preserve it" (Luke 17: 33). Oddly enough as the husband glorifies his wife he also is glorified: he becomes a true man. Once this happens the marriage can potentially be ushered into the final and most wonderful stage of genuine equality, mutual submission, and reciprocity. Here, a husband and wife can discover a whole new world of constantly increasing joy and love. This is no easy road and it might take some time to find it, but it's the only one worth trying for.

The Glorious Woman

It's worth trying for because the glory of a husband and wife are intrinsically linked. As the apostle Paul has it elsewhere "woman is the glory of man" (1 Corinthians 11: 7). If I really want to know what sort of husband a husband is, I need look no further than his wife. A confident, flourishing, joyful wife is obviously a woman much loved by her husband.

Indeed a husband's glory can only rise to the degree he glorifies his wife. Her glory is his, his glory, hers.

But the corollary is just as true: the *un*-glorified wife *de*-glorifies her husband. An abused, neglected or unloved wife soon reflects her diminished glory back on her husband. Bitterness, anger, resentment, coldness and open contempt accompany the un-loved, un-glorified woman. Even her health and physical appearance can be affected if she is not glorified by her husband.

This is not only true in marriage. It can affect whole communities, countries and cultures as well. I believe the way men in a particular community treat the women of that community will in turn influence the overall level of glory that community can rise to. It is a well-known fact that many charities and non-government organizations have discovered that the best way to develop a disadvantaged community is to primarily spend the money on the women in preference to the men. As one United Nations reports states, "Gender Equality is essential for growth and poverty reduction."[xxxv] Since the 1970s, studies have consistently shown that empowering women is indispensable for bringing a community out of poverty and promoting effective social change.

The Glorified Husband

Only a man who is secure in love has any chance of really glorifying his wife. A man who submits himself to the love of God will be much more capable of genuinely serving his wife. Just as Christ loves the church in the same way he is loved by the Father, so too the husband will be able to love his wife as he realizes and submits to the love of God.

Okay — enough about husbands! Women have an equal share of responsibility in the marriage relationship too. It's a different kind of responsibility but it's just as vital to the mutual glorification of both parties in the marriage.

Understanding Submission

I talked with a woman once who had been brutally abused by her former husband for over a decade. She told me of the many times she had been hospitalised with broken bones and bruises after her husband had finished with her. Not only did he break her body; he also broke her spirit. Her whole life was closely controlled and minutely monitored. She was constantly criticised, belittled and shouted at. If she stepped out of line she could expect a severe scolding and the back of his hand — if she was lucky. She was being systematically crushed. Eventually she could take it no more and secretly escaped with her children to the safety of a friend's house.

Later she sought the counsel of a well-known minister hoping he might provide some insight and a way to rebuild her life. Unbelievably he advised her to go back to her husband and 'submit' to him. "It's God's will" he insisted. Incredibly she did what the minister demanded, but nothing had changed and it wasn't long before she was back in hospital yet again. Happily she has since permanently separated from her abusive husband and her life is now wonderfully restored and joyous. But the thing that really infuriates me in this story — apart from the abusive husband — is the ill-informed and reckless advice of the minister.

Unfortunately that's not the first nor the last time I have heard such a story. As explained above, this kind of faulty advice is based on an entirely mistaken view of the Apostle Paul's words about submission.

The word 'submission' is not popular these days — or any days for that matter. We have an inbuilt prejudice against submission mainly due to our exposure to abusive authority. This has led us to believe that submission is equivalent to inferiority. So, the subject of submission gets silently shelved and few, it seems, are willing to seriously talk about it.

I remember one time, shortly before a church meeting, the minister approached me and asked, "What are you speaking about today?"

To which I replied, "I thought we might open up the whole subject of submission in marriage."

The minister suddenly became very grave, placed a hand on my shoulder and drilled me with his eyes. "I've always liked you David. It's a pity you're going to be dead in less than an hour."

It's a little bit funny I suppose, but at another level it's not funny at all.

A Model of Submission

As always, if we want to get a proper understanding of authentic submission it won't do us much good to look at the broken role models we're so familiar with. Instead — as you might now have come to expect — we must take a long look at Jesus Christ. As Christ submits to the Father, so the church is to submit to Christ, and the wife to the husband. Jesus teaches us about true headship and true submission all at once.

As previously explained in Chapter Three, Jesus didn't see submission as inferiority; it was his delight to submit to the Father because he knew he was deeply loved and equal with his Father in every respect. Jesus lost nothing in his submission; on the contrary he was glorified as he did the will of his Father. Of course Jesus knew that the will of his Father was only for good and mutually beneficial. It's out of this secure place that Jesus is then able to freely love and serve his bride, the Church. All he expects is that we, in turn, will submit to his love: that we will let ourselves be glorified by him.

Let me explain how this works with a very loose translation of the latter part of the story where Jesus had begun to wash his disciples' feet in John 13: 5-8. When Jesus came to wash Peter's feet, Peter stopped him, incredulous that he, the Lord and master, would serve him in such a lowly way. Peter said, "Lord, what on earth do you think you're doing? Are *you* really going to wash *my* feet?"

Jesus replied, "I know you don't understand what I am doing for you right now, but later it will make sense."

Peter resisted all the more, "No way," he said, "I'll never let *you* wash *my* feet."

Jesus answered, "Unless you let me wash you, unless you let me serve you, then you'll have no part with me."

Can you see what's going on here? Peter must understand that unless he submits to the love and service of Christ he will never really participate in the ongoing flow of love. The first and most important act of faith is not *us* loving Christ, rather it's submitting to *his* love for us. Notice in the passage from Ephesians, it's the groom who makes the bride glorious. It's not for the Church to make herself glorious so that she can be accepted by Christ. It's the other way around! Christ accepts us as we are, then he washes us, and loves us into our glory "to present her to himself as a radiant church" (Ephesians 5: 27). All Christ asks of us is to submit to his washing — his love, his grace, his mercy.

Real Submission

That's the kind of template Paul is using to measure submission. He's certainly *not* saying that the husband is the 'boss' of his wife. Sure, a husband is meant to be first in line to serve, but a wife is not subordinate to her husband. What he *is* saying is this: wives, do not resist the love of your husbands, rather let them freely glorify and serve you, and respond in kind. Real submission is all about receiving and responding to the initiative of self-giving love. You might be thinking to yourself, "That doesn't sound too difficult," but just like when Peter resisted the washing of his feet, it's a whole lot harder than it looks. We've already seen some of the obvious faults of men, but if women have a fault then it's this: resisting glorification.

I've had many a conversation with an exasperated husband who, having finally understood what it means to share his advantage with his wife, wants nothing more than to see his wife flourish and grow, but no matter how hard he tries his wife simply won't believe a single word of encouragement or think herself worthy of such love.

I talked with a man, who we'll call Michael, who had come into a magnificent realisation of the love of God and his life was turned upside-down. It wasn't long before his attitude to his wife Susan — and women in general — was radically altered. He desperately wanted to make up for lost time in his marriage and set out to truly love and serve his wife, but Susan — rather than receiving his attentions with gladness — was unnerved and threatened by them instead. Then, oddly enough, the relationship turned sour for some time as Susan beat a hasty retreat from Michael's attempts to love her. "I don't understand what's going on? Why won't she let me love her?" Michael pleaded.

Talking with Susan it soon became clear. She was simply unprepared for love. Deep down, she wanted nothing more than the very thing Michael was now offering her, but over the years she'd developed a certain satisfaction in the knowledge that she, at least, had been keeping her end of the marriage 'bargain' faithfully. She'd settled for second best and made the most of her lot in life. They were wealthy enough, and their children were wonderful, and life wasn't all that bad. Sure, the marriage wasn't everything it could be, but that was hardly her fault, she reasoned. Now Michael's radical reformation was forcing her to respond: forcing her to grow. For the first time, the ball actually came back over the net, and Susan had completely forgotten how to swing a racquet.

At first Susan thought it would be a temporary thing that would soon pass — but it didn't. Michael was serious and she had to admit he was different. Now the searchlight was on her, and all the things she had long been able to ignore came to the foreground. Even Michael's compliments were confronting. Whenever he admired her or praised her, all she could see were her imperfections and shortcomings. When he asked her what she really wanted out of life she had to admit she didn't really know; she'd never really thought about it before. As one of several girls in her family she wasn't used to being the centre of attention. Being genuinely loved wasn't what she thought it would be like — all those ridiculous romantic comedies didn't prepare her for this! Susan was being confronted with the chance to grow up and become a real woman.

The only way this can possibly happen in any marriage is if the wife summons the courage to freely submit to her husband's love, and be willing to take up an equal share of the power being offered to her. It requires courage because there are no longer any barriers and disadvantages to hide behind. The excuses for not becoming all she could be are removed. With an equal playing field comes the freedom to be all that she can be, including equal decision-making, equal responsibility and equal accountability. It takes a real woman to do something like that — until then she remains a girl.

Completing the circle

Once a woman is able to let herself be loved then the circle is complete, and glory can flow freely back and forth between husband and wife. The more the wife is glorified, the more she is able to respect and glorify her husband, who in turn has more capacity to glorify his wife, which then enables her to glorify her husband all the more, and on it goes in an endless cycle of mutual glorification.

I remember a game I used to play as a child called 'stacking hands' where a group of children sat around a table and each child would take turns to place their hand on top of the pile of hands in the middle of the table. Once it got going it would develop into a riotous flurry and a rapidly revolving cycle of hands moving from top to bottom. It's not a game you win or lose — it's just for fun! Similarly marriage can ultimately become a rapidly revolving cycle of giving and receiving, of love responding to love, where both husband and wife have an equal share of power and responsibility. Ultimately, husband and wife end up equally submitting to one another (Ephesians 5: 21) and it becomes impossible to discover where the love starts or ends. Marriage isn't a hierarchy; it's a mutuality of glory.

Forgiveness and Responsibility

Of course if you're anything like me, you're imperfect and broken and all this can seem like an impossible aspirational dream. But, glorification is not a destination: rather, we are becoming what we are, and along the way both husband and wife need the humility to admit fault and the grace to forgive one another. There's an old seventies movie called "Love story" which is infamously remembered for a single sentence, "Love means never having to say you're sorry." Anyone who is married knows this is blatantly untrue. Love means saying sorry often and constantly; and forgiving just as often and just as constantly.

Just as importantly, the husband or the wife must be responsible for their own part in the marriage and not wait until their spouse 'behaves properly' before they act. When a husband says, "If she respects me then I'll lay down my life for her," or the wife says, "If he finally learns how to really love me, then I'll submit to him," then the end result will always be a stalemate (or should I say two stalemates).

It takes courage, responsibility and a whole lot of grace to make a marriage flourish. Only then is there space to grow and gradually become our true selves.

Marriage isn't easy, but when it does go right it can be a beautiful reflection of the love between Father, Son and Holy Spirit. That's got to be worth growing into.

12

GLORY AND FAMILY

Mutual Glory – Parents and Children

The delightful movie "Billy Elliot" follows a year in the life of Billy, an eleven year old boy from a tough coal mining town in England during the miners' strikes of the mid-eighties. Billy lived with his coal miner father and older brother, his mother having died some time before. The drama begins with Billy brawling clumsily and unsuccessfully in the boxing ring at the local gymnasium. Billy is less than average as a boxer, and before long he becomes increasingly fascinated with the ballet lessons held in another section of the same gymnasium.

Eventually, Billy secretly joins the ballet group where he soon discovers his passion to dance. All the while his father had no idea what he is up to. Inevitably Billy is caught out by his father. "Lads," says Billy's father in a scornful voice, "do football or boxing... not *ballet!*" and he forbids Billy from attending the classes ever again. Even so, Billy secretly goes on taking private lessons from the ballet teacher.

Then one night, while Billy demonstrates his dancing prowess to a friend at the gymnasium, his father unexpectedly chanced upon him and for the first time witnesses Billy in full flight. Billy is undaunted and continues to dance his heart out in front of his father. His father watches for some time and eventually turns on his heel and strides forcefully away. Billy, of course, assumes his father is outraged and will bring an end to his dancing days for ever. Instead, it turns out Billy's father has finally comprehended the full extent of his son's extraordinary gift and is determined to do whatever it takes to help Billy realize his dream. With no money and no work he has little choice but to sell his most treasured possessions — his late wife's jewellery and wedding ring — to give Billy his chance.

The final scene of the movie jumps forward to a decade later and has Billy's father and older brother arriving at a great hall in London just as a performance of 'Swan Lake' is beginning. They're ushered to their seats as the orchestra strikes up. The music swells and all eyes are trained on stage. Billy's father waits. Finally, as the music reaches a crescendo and light floods the stage, Billy enters with a spectacular arcing leap as his father looks on with tears in his eyes bursting with pride.

Glory!

To me this story is a beautiful snapshot of how the earthly relationship between parents and children can reflect — however dimly — the relationship of the Father and the Son.

It may only be an imperfect shadow of the perfect truth —
but so it always is with human parenting.

Mutual Glory

In many ways the same principles that apply to a mutually
glorifying marriage relationship also apply to the relationship
between parents and children. Little wonder then that Paul
goes straight on from writing about marriage in the Ephesians
epistle, to the relationship between parents and children,

> Children, obey your parents in the Lord, for this is right. "Honor
> your father and mother"- which is the first commandment with
> a promise - "so that it may go well with you and that you may
> enjoy long life on the earth." Fathers, do not exasperate your
> children; instead, bring them up in the training and instruction
> of the Lord.
>
> — Ephesians 6: 1-4

Again, both parent and child have different but vital roles
to play in a mutually glorifying relationship.

Glory sensitive

All children *know* they are created for glory, and like
delicate seedlings, they soak up the sunshine of glorification
very easily. I remember admiring the mental ability of one
of my nieces when she was aged about three saying, "You
know you're a *very* clever girl."

To which she replied with a beaming smile "I know! And
you should see me when I run!"

Then off she dashed to demonstrate the truth of her assertion. There was no hint of conceit in her reply; she was just innocently enjoying being in her own skin.

However, small children are just as vulnerable to the frosts of de-glorification. I once saw a little boy balancing on a narrow curb on the roadside intent on demonstrating his new-found dexterity and enjoying his boyish exuberance. Walking behind him, his mother continuously shouted at him, "Get down off of there! You're only going to fall over and dirty your clothes and wreck everything like you always do! You can't do anything right so stop it!" I could almost see the little boy's soul being crushed and could pretty much predict the probable pathway his life would take. You don't have to be a psychologist to wind back the clock and imagine the kind of parenting the boy's mother had received as a child.

The way parents treat their children can have ramifications for generations to come — both for good and ill. I find it fascinating that my long-dead, great-great-grandparents are still having an ongoing effect on my life, and the life of my children here and now. This glory stuff turns out to be kind of important.

Unique Glory

Paul begins his advice to parents with, "do not exasperate your children," or put in other words; don't frustrate them, thereby provoking them to anger and hopelessness, but "instead bring them up in the training and instruction of the Lord." The phrase 'bring them up' can correctly be translated as nurture, promote, or strengthen. This verse could therefore be paraphrased as "nurture, promote, and strengthen them; bring out the best in them, enabling them to become everything they can be following the way of the Lord."

How can a parent do this for their children? The simple answer is to love them. Specifically: to love them in a way that will unlock their hidden potential. There's no 'one-size-fits-all' way to love a child, as each child is unique. Parents who desire to treat all their children equally soon discover it may be necessary to therefore treat each one differently. As it is in Proverbs, "Give a lad training *suitable to his character* and, even when old, he will not go back on it" (Proverbs 22: 6 New Jerusalem Bible). In other words, train up the child according to *who he or she essentially is*, not according to the way you want them to go.

When parents pressure their children to be something, or do something 'unsuitable to their character' the outcome is nearly always ill-fated. Like the athletic dad pushing his un-sporty son to excel at football, or an academic mum pressuring her daughter to attempt a university degree she has no chance of completing, or the wistful farmer who expects his oldest son — who has no interest in agriculture — to take on the family farm. In each of these examples, the inevitable outcome is an 'exasperated child.'

It's not for parents to fashion their children in their own image, or impose their own aspirations upon them, but rather to discover, nurture and unfurl the unique and particular character of their children — to glorify *them*.

Building a bond

Nurturing the potential in a child is a complicated, multifaceted, life-long pursuit and it takes a whole lot more than good food, a warm bed and a decent education to raise a secure child. Children intuitively know whether they are genuinely loved or not and no amount of money or gifts can make up for unfettered time and actual relationship. All that other stuff plays a distant second.

The most important thing parents can teach their children is what a truly loving relationship looks like *from the inside of one*.

Children come to know themselves as they are known and learn to love as they are loved. They need to know that they are loved for *who they are*, not for how they behave or what they do. This kind of love takes time: time to carefully observe, to listen to, to interact with, to protect, to teach, and — most important of all — to simply *be* with the child.

The pattern of emotional interaction established between parent and child in the early years tends to set the child's expectations for all future relationships. Most of what they learn about relating to others is 'caught' from their parents. For this reason, children need their parents to be consistent in unconditional love. Statements such as, "After all I've done for you, this is how you treat me?" or "Why can't you behave better and be more like your sister?," only engender an insecure 'contractual' basis of relationship. If a child grows up believing that love has to be earned in some way it can significantly affect how he or she will view God.

Parenting, and the Image of God

Perhaps this is why Paul puts "not exasperating the child" before "bringing them up in the training and instruction of the Lord" (Ephesians 6: 1-4). A child's relationship with their parents is where they gain their first 'image of God.' A child who is genuinely loved is predisposed to seeing God as loving and trustworthy. Of course the opposite is true for a child who hasn't experienced authentic love. He or she sees the world as an unsafe place and suspects God is not to be trusted and is therefore less likely to submit to the "training and instruction of the Lord."

Over the years I've heard many a youth say to me in anger, "If God is 'Father' — as you say — then I don't want anything to do with him! My father was a cruel tyrant!" or words to that effect. I talked with one young woman who went so far as saying "My father's not really my father. To me he's just a sperm-donor." A harsh assessment, but perhaps not completely unwarranted, after all. Genuine fatherhood or motherhood is a relational truth, not just a biological fact. A child who has experienced emotionally disconnected parenting may be able to acknowledge God as Creator or Lord, but will probably struggle to see God as 'Father.'

Glory Deficits

To some degree this is true of *everybody*. We've all been brought up in an imperfect world by imperfect parents (I know for certain that my children have a somewhat flawed father to cite one example). I've had countless conversations with both men and women who are stuck in the mire of their less than perfect childhood memories. Their stories vary enormously, but they all have a common theme. Every one of them felt that they hadn't received the kind of love and connection they needed to secure them as worthwhile, loveable, human beings. It's an unavoidable and universal fact that we've all experienced a fundamental mismatch between what we know we are created to be and what our experience tells us we are.

This mismatch eventually forms a kind of fault-line in our souls. I remember taking an excursion with my school geography class many years ago to some arid mountains north of the city where I lived at the time. We had the opportunity to investigate a fault-line in the sedimentary layers of an ancient cliff. At some point in the prehistoric past, powerful seismic movements in the earth's crust had caused an immense chunk of earth to slip away from the rest of the mountain. The fault line was obvious as the different coloured layers of horizontal sediment were massively mismatched along an extensive diagonal fracture in the rock.

Seismic movements such as trauma, abuse, neglect and rejection can also cause massive mismatches between our internal sense of inherent self-worth and our actual experience of the world around us — most especially in our relationship with our parents. When this happens it creates a 'glory deficit.' The greater the mismatch, the greater the deficit.

Glory deficits are nearly impossible to ignore. Glory is so fundamental to our identity and wellbeing that we will subconsciously try to reconcile our deficit by either filling the hole in our soul with 'self-glorification,' or comforting ourselves with 'self-medication.'

Self-glorification can take the form of perfectionism, self-righteousness, greed, manipulation, narcissism, bullying, hyper-spirituality and a host of other unhappy arrangements. Self-medication is more likely to express itself in some kind of addiction to drugs, alcohol, food, excitement, gambling or sex. Sometimes we mix and match. In the end, these responses are completely futile and self-destructive, to say nothing of the collateral damage we inflict on those around us.

If the strain and pain of trying to fix our glory deficit is not addressed, it inevitably leads to a breakdown of some sort, which may reveal itself in all kinds of disorders such as anxiety, depression, dissociative syndromes, an identity crisis and a host of other mental and physical illnesses too complex to cover here.

Whatever the external symptoms may be, there can be no healing until the internal drivers of the deficit such as shame, guilt, alienation, grief, anger and sorrow, are wholly and deeply addressed. Until then, the deficit continues to provide momentum to a self-perpetuating downward spiral.

Real Life Glory Deficits

Glory deficits are like cancer to the soul and just like cancer they can manifest themselves in many different forms. I once talked with a man in his middle thirties who we'll call 'Frank' who had been brought up by wealthy, well-meaning, but emotionally distant parents. The only times they did show any approval or affection toward him was when he had achieved exceptional grades at school.

Consequently, Frank began to throw himself into his academic studies with an enthusiasm that bordered on fanatical. If Frank's grades were anything below the highest possible standard, he would plunge into depression and self-recrimination and then redouble his efforts. For the most part he excelled well beyond the standards that even his parents demanded of him. Unsurprisingly, in his early adult life he struggled with perfectionistic and workaholic tendencies that affected his marriage and family.

Frank applied a similar misplaced enthusiasm to his spirituality, believing his acceptance by 'God' was based on his moral performance, piety and acts of service. Inevitably Frank could not maintain the weight of his own expectations and he suffered a debilitating emotional breakdown — or perhaps it was a breakthrough? Whatever the case, this was a turning point in Frank's life and through it he began to discover that God — at least — loved him for who he was and not for his moral attainments or extravagant service. Frank has since begun to gradually 'unlearn' the pattern of acceptance he learned from his parents.

On another occasion I talked at length with a woman who we'll call 'Judith' who was raised in a family with her four sisters by parents who were simply unavailable either physically or emotionally. Being the youngest in the family meant Judith was often overlooked and missed out on significant family events. Judith felt alone even in a crowded house and she craved the affection and attention of her parents. Judith soon learned if she really wanted to get their attention, then all she needed to do was grossly misbehave, or run away from home. All of a sudden her parents would give her their full attention; albeit negative attention; but at least she was being noticed.

In her late teens Judith discovered that men were more than happy to give her all the 'affection' and 'attention' she could hope for and before long she immersed herself in a series of unhappy liaisons and failed affairs. Now in her middle thirties, Judith still suffers from frequent anxiety attacks, depression, suicidal feelings and an eating disorder. In addition, she has trouble trusting people in general and men in particular.

Stories such as this can be multiplied endlessly, and in many cases, much more horribly. This is not to say that damaged children are always the result of poor parenting, but what we can say is that children who do not feel loved and known by their parents will be significantly more vulnerable to the debilitating effects of a glory deficit.

Only Jesus

One of the problems with glory deficits is that they cannot be entirely healed by any human therapy. We're all a bit like Humpty Dumpty of nursery rhyme fame,

> Humpty Dumpty sat on a wall,
> Humpty Dumpty had a great fall,
> All the king's horses,
> And all the king's men,
> Couldn't put Humpty together again.

For 'king's men' here, insert: counsellor, preacher, psychologist and medical practitioner. There's no one who has the wisdom or the power to reverse the seismic movements that created the deficit in the first place. They may be able to help us or diagnose us; but ultimately they can't actually heal us.

Even our parents don't have the capacity to give us what we really need. They might have pointed us in the right direction, or they may have even loved us as well as it is possible for a human being to love — but we need something more.

At some point we must look past our parents to Jesus Christ to find our true identity and ultimate healing. He is the only one who has the capacity to reconfigure the tectonic plates of a human soul. By becoming human and taking on our shame and guilt, and the pain of our broken humanity, Jesus has accomplished what no one else can even imagine, much less do. He has realigned the mismatched markers in our souls. Through the incarnation, culminating in the cross and the resurrection, Jesus Christ has annihilated our deficits to present us 'without stain or wrinkle or any other blemish, but holy and blameless' before the Father (Ephesians 5: 27).

It's upon this foundation of grace that it becomes possible for imperfect children to truly honor their imperfect parents, and for imperfect parents to truly love their imperfect children. Jesus Christ restores our souls and gives both parent and child the grace and space to live, love and forgive.

The Responsible Child

In the end we can't blame our parents for the outcome of our lives. We're responsible for ourselves, no matter what our family of origin was like. Hence Paul's unqualified instruction in the Ephesian passage to children, "Honor your father and mother" — which is the first commandment with a promise — "so that it may go well with you and that you may enjoy long life on the earth" (Ephesians 6:2-3). This statement has its origin in the Ten Commandments, where the word 'honor' is the same word used elsewhere in the Old

Testament for glory (Deuteronomy 5: 16). Paul is therefore instructing children to glorify their parents, *regardless of their shortcomings.*

If we cannot honor our parents then it's as certain as night follows day 'that it will *not* go well with [us].' If we are at war with our parents then we are at war with ourselves and like all wars, there can be no true winner.

I once had a conversation with a young man who was the son of a well-known evangelical preacher. At that time he was a drug-addict and openly confessed to being involved in satanic rituals. "What made you want to do that?" I asked.

He shot back with obvious venom in his voice "To get back at my father for putting the church before me."

Whatever he was doing it was having the desired effect — but at what cost to himself?

Sadly, the incidence of adult children who deliberately sabotage their own glory as a way of de-glorifying their parents is all too common, but it's a self-defeating way to live. When we dishonor our parents, we dishonor ourselves. There's really nothing good to come from it.

Forgiveness and Gratitude

On the other hand, when we honor our parents — no matter how apparently undeserving they may *seem* to be — we bring dignity to ourselves. *The least honor we can give is to forgive.* Forgiveness means freeing the other person of their debts: in this case, the debt of love. Only then can we take true responsibility for our own lives. This, of course, is never easy, and may even be the hardest thing we'll ever do — especially if we happen to be carrying around a larger than normal glory deficit. Forgiveness doesn't mean you have to trust the forgiven person: it just cancels the debts of the past.

Naturally when we mature into adulthood, we may come to recognise just how difficult and complicated it is to be a parent. This can be a crucial time of turnaround in our attitude toward our parents that may set the stage for a deeper appreciation for all the things our parents have *actually* done for us — no matter what their shortcomings.

Gratitude is one of most powerful ways of bringing honor to parents. I have talked with many elderly parents who long to hear the simple words, 'thank you' coming from the mouths of their adult children. Sadly, many go to their graves with those words remaining profoundly unsaid.

Greater Honor

The greatest honor a son or daughter can give to their parents is to simply be the best version of themselves they can be. In exactly the same way the Son glorifies the Father by simply being a glorious son, so children glorify their parents as they shine.

Our youngest son, Max, has a gift for drama and acting. He can squeeze more emotion into a single facial expression than anyone I know. When Max was in pre-school he shared a class with a boy who suffered from acute autism. As a result it was near impossible to communicate with this boy and no one could teach him how to use the bathroom — not even his parents. But Max somehow found a way to break through the communication barrier with sign language and facial expressions and taught the boy how to use the bathroom all by himself.

The next day when I went to pick Max up from pre-school, the autistic child's parents greeted me enthusiastically as they gushed with praise for Max and heaped gratitude on me as well — even though I hadn't done a thing! By simply being himself Max brought honor to himself and also to his parents.

I've observed countless parents bursting with pure pride and overwhelmed with raw emotion as they watch their children running in a race, or graduating from school, or preforming in a drama, or playing a piano, or receiving an award, or starting a new career. The glory of the moment is mutually shared between the parent and the child.

In this way the relationship between parents and children can also become an endless cycle of mutual glorification, as the love of the parents engenders confidence in the child, which propels the child to even greater heights, which in turn promotes even more delight from the parents — and on it goes, from glory, to glory, to glory.

Glory in Every Relationship

This is how it has always been from before creation with the Father, Son and Holy Spirit, in continuous, mutual-glorification, and never-ending, selfless love, which has overflowed to the rest of creation. The glory of their love is the basis of every relationship that can be named.

This kind of 'mutual-glorification' has the capacity to change not only families and friendships, but whole communities and nations. What a world it would be if every relationship was rooted in the ground of this truth; a world where the rich cared for the poor, the healthy for the sick, the free for the oppressed and the powerful for the weak.

It would be heaven on earth! That's precisely what glory is all about.

This is what we're praying for every time we recite the words of the Lord's Prayer, "your kingdom come, your will be done, on earth as it is in heaven" (Matthew 6: 10). As we submit to glorification from God, we have the grace to give glory to one another, which in turn glorifies God, and all along the Lord's Prayer is becoming a reality.

Isaiah gives us a glimpse of just what that might look like,

> What I'm interested in seeing you do is:
> sharing your food with the hungry,
> inviting the homeless poor into your homes,
> putting clothes on the shivering ill-clad,
> being available to your own families.
> Do this and the lights will turn on,
> and your lives will turn around at once.
> Your righteousness will pave your way.
> The GOD of glory will secure your passage.
> Then when you pray, GOD will answer.
> You'll call out for help and I'll say, 'Here I am.'
> — Isaiah 58: 6-9 (The Message).

This is the hope of glory being fulfilled.
It starts here.
It starts now.
It starts with you.

ACKNOWLEDGEMENTS

It is a well-known truism that there is no such thing as an original thought: the only thing that's original is the unique combination of un-original thoughts that exists in each person. This is particularly true as far as this author is concerned. There are more people than I can possibly remember to whom I am indebted for making this book possible.

To my wife Catherine, the wisest and the most long-suffering woman I know — thankyou. To my four spectacular children, Tait, Tess, Jack, and Max — you are my joy and glory — thank you for the many illustrations you have provided. Thanks also belongs to my parents, Dennis and Dawn, for their godly example and faithful love.

I am also profoundly grateful to all the members of the two churches I have had the privilege of serving, — *Port Hacking Community Church* in Sydney, and *The Fish Gate Uniting Church* in Adelaide — thank you for letting me walk with you.

I am grateful to the late Geoffrey Bingham for pointing me toward the grace of God and introducing me to Christian theology, to Barry Chant who taught me about the reality of the Holy Spirit, and to Baxter Kruger for opening my mind to a bigger vision of Jesus Christ (and also for your friendship and humble spirit whenever we fish together). Thank you to Ian Pennicook for introducing me to T. F. Torrance, also to David Mc Gregor for unravelling the mysteries of Karl Barth, and a big thank you to the Perichoresis Australia team — your encouragement and insight has been invaluable

I'd also like to mention those who have specifically added their insights and considerations to help progress this book. Thank you to Amanda Hancock, Baxter Kruger, Bruce Wauchope, Catherine Kowalick, David McGregor, David Walters, Elise Ruthenbeck, Jonathan Wright, Ken Blue, Kristy Schubert, Mark Stevens, Michaela Wauchope, Nicole Dunkley, Patti Blue and Sarah Wauchope, for your literary, editing, graphic art, researching, proofreading and typesetting skills. Special thanks to Jonathan Schubert for your unique encouragement.

In faith — David Kowalick

ENDNOTES

[i]C.S. Lewis – *The Weight of Glory*. Touchstone, New York. 1980. p36

[ii]Romans 8: 21 Revised Authorised Version

[iii]Romans 8: 21 New American Standard Bible

[iv]Kruger, C. B. – 2012. *The Shack Revisited*. Faith Words, NY, USA. p63.

[v]Athanasius, *Contra Ar.* 1.34

[vi]John 13: 31-32 *The Message*

[vii]Sea snakes are venomous but unaggressive and their fangs are small and obscured. Nevertheless don't do this at home.

[viii]*Against Heresies* Book IV, Chapter 20, 7

[ix]Inspired by Karl Barth and David McGregor.

[x]Inspired by T.F. Torrance.

[xi]NIV Study Bible1985, Zondervan, p1899

[xii]D. Martyn Lloyd-Jones, *Joy unspeakable*, Eastbourne Kingsway184,p80

[xiii]Dr. Arthur Janov, instigator of 'primal therapy'- referred to by G. Bingham.

[xiv]Romans 8: 17 – Young's.

[xv]Bingham Geoffrey. *God's Glory Man's Sexuality*. NCPI, Blackwood SA. 1988. P13

[xvi]Powerful angelic beings

[xvii]Inspired by Geoff Bingham

[xviii]Lord Tennyson. A. – *In Memoriam A.H.H.* 1849 (poem).

[xix]C.S. Lewis – *The Weight of Glory*. Touchstone, New York. 1980. p36

[xx]The Book of Common Prayer – Oxford University Press, Oxford England. 1938. p198.

[xxi]Bingham Geoffrey. *Love's most glorious covenant*. Redeemer Baptist Press. Castle Hill, Australia. 1997. P38-39

[xxii]C.S. Lewis – *The Weight of Glory*. Touchstone, New York. 1980. p28

[xxiii]D.G. Cooper - *Death of the Family*. Pantheon Books, New York. 1971.

[xxiv]T. F. Torrance, *Trinitarian Faith: The Evangelical theology of the Ancient Catholic Church*, T & T Clark, NY, USA, 1997. P134

[xxv]T. F. Torrance – *The Mediation of Christ*, 1992. T&T Clark, p40.

[xxvi]Gregory Nazianzus - *Nicene and Post Nicene Fathers*, Vol 2, #7, p. 648, at www.ccel.org (Gregory was actually referring to Jesus assuming the fallen human mind here, but the principle remains valid for every aspect of our fallen humanity).

[xxvii]T. F. Torrance - *Theology in Reconstruction* (London 1965) pp 159-160

[xxviii]Kruger, C. B. – 2012. *The Shack Revisited*. Faith Words, NY, USA. p223

[xxix]For a fuller insight into these matters I suggest N. T. Wright's book on the subject: *Surprised by Hope* 2007. SPCK London

[xxx]Lewis C.S. – *Surprised by Joy*. 2002. Harper-Collins, London UK p22

[xxxi]Ibid – p17

[xxxii]ABC Television – *Q&A*, November 7, 2011

[xxxiii]United Nations report, "Long-standing inequalities in the gender distribution of economic and financial resources have placed women at a disadvantage relative to men in their capability to participate in, contribute to and benefit from broader processes of development." Aavailable at: www.un.org/womenwatch/daw/public/WorldSurvey2009.pdf accessed March 2012

[xxxiv]Stromquist N. P. – 2007 *The Gender Socialization Process in Schools*: A Cross-National Comparison - available at http://unesdoc.unesco.org/images/0015/001555/155587e.pdf - accessed March 2012

[xxxv]UN Commission of the European Communities, *Communication from the Commission to the European Parliament and Council: Gender Equality and Women Empowerment in Development Cooperation*. Accessed http://eyr-lex.europa.eu/LexUriServ/site/en/2007/com2007_0100en01.pdf 12:00 07/04/2012